TEN GOLDEN RULES

OF HORSE TRAINING

Universal Laws for all
Training Levels and Riding Styles

BRUCE NOCK, PH.D.

Half Halt Press, Inc.
Boonsboro, Maryland

TEN GOLDEN RULES OF HORSE TRAINING
Universal Laws for all Training Levels and Riding Styles

© 2004 Bruce Nock, Ph.D.

Published in the United States of America by:

The Specialist Equestrian Publisher
P.O., Box 67
Boonsboro, MD 21713

Photographs by Jean Putz, Dr. Lynn O'Connor
and Dr. Bruce Nock

Illustrations by Diann Landau

Book and Cover Design and Production by:
Design Point Studio

Cover Artwork by Hannah Howard

Ten Golden Rules of Horse Training is intended for educational purposes, to help the reader better understand principles and methods of horse training. However, no book—this one included—can possibly cover or anticipate every possible action a horse might take. Horses are, after all, individuals. Accordingly, neither the author nor the publisher has liability or responsibility for any actions arising from the information shared in this book.

ISBN 0-939481-67-7

TEN GOLDEN RULES

OF HORSE TRAINING

To Moment,

A kind and gentle soul ... my friend.

Bruce Nock

C O N T E N T S

ACKNOWLEDGEMENTS

My parents aren't "horse people." We never owned horses when I was growing up. But I fondly remember family outings on rented horses. I rode Duke. Those short excursions on horseback were the fountainhead of my love of horses.

My friend Jenny Jenkins rekindled my interest in riding and introduced me to training. Jenny passed away years before I began to write this book but it would never have been written had I not met her.

Jean Putz is my buddy, best friend and riding partner. Jean and I share the responsibilities and joys of Watershed Farm. We've learned about horses together for the past 8 years. Her encouragement and support were crucial to the completion of this book and her comments about its style and contents pointed me in the right direction. Jean also helped take photographs for the book—a task that was not inherently appealing to me but which was made much more enjoyable by her participation.

I am indebted to my good friend Lynn O'Connor, Ph.D. Lynn and I were graduate students together at the Institute of Animal Behavior, Rutgers University. Over the years, Lynn and I have spent countless hours discussing endless aspects of animal behavior. The unique perspectives and astute insights Lynn often brought to those discussions contributed greatly to my growth as a horseman and animal behaviorist. Lynn also helped in the early training of Gabriel Oak who I refer to a number of times for practical examples in this book. I also thank Lynn for her valuable comments on early versions of this manuscript.

Cynthia Spaulding, ACRI, deserves recognition. Cindy is the most learned and experienced horseperson I know. She is the person I turn to for discussion when I'm uncertain or puzzled about something pertaining to riding. Her evaluation of an early version of the manuscript was extremely important to me.

I owe a debt of gratitude to Yvonne Eddy, Ph.D., and Richard Forsythe, M.S., of Purdue University—great riding pals who I value highly. We've spent many hours around campfires and kitchen tables telling horse tales. Nevertheless, it isn't easy to turn over an unfinished manuscript to such educated friends, especially when one of them has a Ph.D. in English literature, but I'm glad I did. Bonnie and Dick provided significant insights after reading an early version of the manuscript. I heeded Bonnie's advice concerning writing style to the best of my ability.

I am grateful to all of the people who have allowed me to help them with their horses over the years. They provided opportunities for me to broaden my perspective and grow as a teacher. A special thanks to my friends Gingy Briner and Sherry Crisp who also read an earlier manuscript. Their comments were very helpful in guiding decisions about what to emphasize, expand and clarify.

Thanks to my neighbor and friend, Dorothy Hawk,

who happily gave me free access to her round pen for photographs.

Stacey Wigmore is a cracker-jack copy editor. She told me where to punctuate and where to put spaces, em dashes, etc. She put the polish on the form and format.

Last but certainly not least, I thank my partner in the publication of this book, Elizabeth Carnes, publisher of Half Halt Press. I liked Beth immediately. She seemed very personable—struck me as an unpretentious person who could be counted on and trusted. That proved to be true. Beth unerringly guided me through the book publishing process and even made it enjoyable.

PREFACE

There is an old saying: "No two books are ever exactly alike." It isn't meant to be taken at face value. The term "book" is actually a metaphor for "individuals." The saying is a similitude for individual differences. Nevertheless, there is truth to the statement even when taken literally. For example, it is very unusual to find different books with the same title. But books can differ from one another in many other ways, as well: cover design, page layout, type style, paper quality, and so on. Different books also don't usually have the same number of pages, and sometimes pages are numbered with Roman numerals, while other times Arabic numbers are used. Some books have line drawings and photographs, others have one but not the other type of illustration, while still others have neither. Some books have prefaces, acknowledgements and/or indexes, others do not.

Nevertheless, despite seemingly endless differences between books, you and I usually can read all of them. Why? Because we understand certain basic rules of reading! If the book is written in English, we know to read it from front to back, pages from top to bottom and lines from left to right.

There is really nothing mysterious or complex about it; differences like cover design, page layout, etc. are inconsequential to the process of reading a book.

You are probably wondering what this has to do with training horses. It might surprise you but, in one respect, training horses is much like reading a book. There are basic rules that can guide one's actions regardless of the details of the situation. Unfortunately, all too often when training horses we get bogged down worrying about superficial differences rather than looking more deeply for commonalities. It's a case of becoming so absorbed with the differences between trees that we overlook the fact that they are all part of the same forest.

I once heard a student ask an instructor what to do when a horse shies. The instructor replied, "That is a difficult problem, and the optimal reaction depends on the exact circumstances, the horse's temperament and the rapport between rider and horse." At first blush, that might seem like a reasonable answer. The fact is, however, it is equivalent to telling someone who asks how to read a book that it depends on the cover design, number of pages, type style, and so on. There is no way that such information will help anyone read a book. Likewise, the instructor's reply certainly did nothing to prepare the student for handling a horse when it shies. Even worse, the student probably was somewhat discouraged—the instructor's response certainly makes it sound like managing an apprehensive horse is a complex and situationally dependent matter.

In the chapters that follow, I describe 10 golden rules that are based on modern behavioral and learning theory.

The golden rules apply to all styles of riding and to all levels of training, from the most basic to the most advanced. They are not difficult to comprehend and, once you understand them, you will see that it is the equivalent of knowing how to go about reading a book. The golden rules are the foundation for training horses gently and tactfully. They will guide your actions and reactions regardless of a horse's temperament, experience and exact circumstances. It is only when one does not understand the golden rules that each training situation seems different from every other.

C H A P T E R

I N T R O D U C T I O N

You Might Need to Know Less
Than You Think to Train Horses

Xenophon was a Greek cavalry general who commanded 10,000 horsemen during the last of the Peloponnesian Wars. He lived from about 430 BC to about 355 BC. He wrote *The Art of Horsemanship*—the oldest surviving book on the subject.[1] It's a remarkable book that's written in a simple, easy manner and, even though it was written more than 2,000 years ago, it is still in many respects a sound guide for handling horses. For me, the most unexpected aspect of the book is its uncompromising emphasis on tact and gentleness. In one of my favorite passages, Xenophon wrote, "If you desire to handle a good war-horse so as to make his action the more magnificent and striking, you must refrain from pulling at his mouth with the bit as well as from spurring and whipping him. Most people think that this is the way to make him look fine; but they only produce an effect exactly contrary to what they desire."[2] He went on to say that "what the horse does under compulsion ... is done without understanding; and there is no beauty in it either, any more than if one should whip and spur a dancer. There would be a great deal more ungracefulness than beauty in ... a horse that was so treated."[3] Extraordinary pronouncements from a military field commander who lived 2,500 years ago, wouldn't you agree?

Historical accounts indicate that Xenophon was a man of iron will and self-discipline. His very survival in battle was largely dependent on the performance of his horse and on that of the 10,000 men under him. In fact, he wrote, "... a disobedient horse is not only useless, but he often plays the part of a very traitor."[4] Nevertheless, throughout his book he admonishes the use of force in training war horses and strongly advocates kindness. He believed this was the best method for producing a superior war horse that was optimally responsive and obedient. Xenophon needed sure-fire methods that would produce solid, reliable horses that he could count on in battle—stake his life on—and he recognized that tact and gentleness paid the greatest dividends in the long run. That principle remains true today. In the words of the late Portuguese riding master Nuno Oliveira: "Although progress may seem slow, it is only by rational and gentle work that a horse can be called really trained."[5] And, it is just as applicable for training the pleasure horse, the hunter, the jumper, the dressage or the reining horse, etc. as it is for training a war horse.

The truth is, nothing worthwhile results from force. At best, it produces only shallow, superficial results with no enduring value. It is the training method of the ignorant. When you see someone trying to force a horse to do something, conclude that the person lacks the knowledge, skill and understanding to deal with the situation more effectively.

If you are reading this book, I assume that you, like me, are on a mission to gain more information about riding and handling horses, information that will allow you to be more tactful and more effective. Actually, I don't think of it as a mission exactly. A mission, to me, implies a task that can be completed. That's not quite how I see it. It's more like a journey that continues on toward greater understanding and skill. There is always another step to take.

As a scientist, I've learned that each bit of information that's acquired raises more questions than answers. It's part of the attraction of science—new puzzles to ponder, old conclusions to reevaluate, novel experiments to plan. There is always more to discover—dark territory to explore.

Horsemanship follows the same law. The more you learn, the more you discover there is to learn. There is always a higher level of skill and understanding to strive for. The legendary Nuno Oliveira, who the riding elite of the world refer to simply as "The Master," wrote: "I know that I still have much to learn, and will go on learning until my dying day, not only by riding, but by studying, thinking deeply, and observing."[6] We would all do well to follow his lead. Enjoy the journey; make your goal simply to keep improving. Don't become frustrated when progress seems slow. The road is not always smooth and sometimes you will have to backtrack and start over again. Just keep going—one step, then another. Eventually, you'll look back to find that you have traveled a long way. But it takes time. Hopefully, the information in this book will make your journey a little less bumpy and your time with horses more enjoyable.

All Horses Can Be Pleasant to Handle and Ride

I once heard a statistic that impressed me: Only one out of every five people remains involved with horses for more than a year. Of those who do, only one out of five remains involved for more than five years. I'm not certain about the accuracy of this statistic but there is no question that owning a horse can become disheartening.

Economics is certainly one factor that discourages horse owners. Maintaining and caring for a horse is a big monetary commitment. It also requires a large commitment of time, even if you board your horse at a commercial facility. But, time and money are only part of the story. More often than not, owning a horse simply does not live up to expectations.

Many people become involved with horses as a casual pastime. If they keep their horse at home, they might trail ride on Saturday or Sunday. If they board their horse at a commercial stable, they might go to the barn a couple of times a week to ride in the arena or on local trails; maybe they take a riding lesson. It's a break from their daily routine—a brief escape, an opportunity to relax and just enjoy the moment.

Then they discover that all is not as they had envisioned. Maybe the horse just has habits that are annoying: pawing when tied, for example. Or, maybe the horse is more of an adversary than a willing partner: Maybe he drags them around the arena when they lunge him or, maybe they can't get him to move at all on a lunge line. Maybe he doesn't stand still for mounting, putting them in a frustrating and dangerous situation every time they try to mount. Maybe he refuses to move forward without the rider kicking and squeezing with all of their might, exhausting them after a trip or two around the arena. Maybe he doesn't change gaits when asked or changes spontaneously. Maybe he is insensitive to the reins or leans heavily on their hands, making them feel as if they are driving a bus. Maybe he bolts or bucks and scares them half to death. Maybe he shies or spooks at every little thing, an attribute that frightens and infuriates many riders. Maybe he throws a fit when they try to ride him away from the barn or jigs on the way back—not exactly what they had foreseen for a quiet trail ride on a cool autumn morning. These are all common problems that you can see every day in boarding stables, at horse shows, on trail rides, etc. And, it is by no means an exhaustive list of the difficulties that people run into. What was supposed to be a peaceful diversion turns out to be an aggravation that might even be dangerous.

As a result, many people simply give up out of exasperation and trade in the horse for a boat, an ATV or a sofa. Others learn to endure the difficulties and to work around them whenever possible. Maybe they don't ride when she's "in season." Or, maybe they only ride in the arena. Perhaps they can ride outside but only on certain days—maybe when it's not too windy or when neighborhood dogs and cats aren't in the vicinity. Maybe they can trail ride, but only if their horse is in the lead. Maybe they don't canter because the horse gets too "worked up," perhaps because "he was a race horse." They stay within limitations set by the horse. Moreover, they accept the limitations because they see so many others doing the same. They believe that everyone has to put up with the annoying idiosyncrasies of their horse.

Of course, it is perfectly reasonable to avoid situations that could injure you or your horse. In fact, before doing anything new with your horse or with an unfamiliar horse, it is a good idea to ask yourself whether either you or the horse could get hurt if things go poorly. If the answer is yes, I recommend not doing it even if it is something suggested by a professional trainer or a riding instructor. Don't feel that you have to prove your bravery to anyone. If things go badly, it will be you who pays the price.

The age and development of the horse, his level of training and physical fitness and his personality can also limit what is reasonable to ask of a horse. Nevertheless, all mature, healthy horses have the capacity to be pleasant to handle and to ride. They should not be annoying, rude or difficult in any way.

Here is a list of attributes that every horse can and should acquire:

- To come when called or, at least, not run away when approached.

- To lead with little effort from the handler. The horse should go forward, move sideways and back up in response to light cues and without pushing or pulling on the handler.

- To stand quietly for grooming, etc.

- To be calm and responsive on a lunge line.

- To load readily and quietly onto and off of trailers.

- To stand still for mounting and for dismounting.

- To be sensitive to leg and rein aids when ridden at the walk, trot or canter, regardless of the situation. The horse should go forward and backward calmly and with minimal effort from the rider. He should change direction, gait and speed when asked and not otherwise.

For readability, I use male pronouns when referring to horses throughout this book. Please do not take this as a prejudice against the female gender. This book is dedicated to my Arabian mare Moment, who I enjoyed riding for many years.

*These are **minimal** qualities that are reasonable to expect from every horse.* But, horses don't acquire these attributes or attain even higher levels of performance through genetics, osmosis or magic. It requires dedication and effort on your part.

You Don't Have to Be a Prodigy, Sage or Mystic to Train Horses

If you want a horse that is pleasant to be around and easy to handle and ride, you have to teach one to be that way. Sure, you could buy a horse with those attributes or you could have a professional train one for you. I've known quite a few people who have done both. Starting with a horse that is well trained is the best thing for most people. Unfortunately, all too often it's a temporary solution. You may know someone who initially raved about his or her new horse only to send him back for retraining or to trade him in for a "better" horse a year later. Then the cycle repeats with the same problems emerging all over again. Why? Because training is an ongoing process! The performance of even a well-trained horse will deteriorate over time if you don't continuously strive to maintain and improve it.

Unfortunately, for the vast majority of riders, the process of training a horse is shrouded in mystery, appearing to require the transcendental insights of a savant or even mystical powers gained through a lifetime of watching and studying horses. The recent emergence of so-called "horse whisperers" hasn't helped. Moreover, there is a belief that training is a fragile process that could "ruin" a horse for life if done incorrectly. These are all myths. You don't have to be a prodigy or a mystic to train horses. Everyone has the potential capacity to train or retrain a horse so that he is easy to handle and ride. Regular people with no special talents or attributes have been doing it for literally thousands of years—even before Xenophon's time. It is not rocket science, as the saying goes. In fact, you need to know a lot less than you might envision to train horses.

You might doubt the validity of that statement if you have been reading other books and magazine articles about training. They can give the impression that a vast amount of detailed knowledge is needed to train what appears to be an endless number of different things. Often there are step-by-step instructions followed by a list of things that can go wrong and how to deal with them. It can be an imposing amount of information to digest.

Over the years, I've read more than 100 books and countless magazine articles on riding and training. Some described comprehensive systems for training horses to very high levels of performance while others dealt with specific individual behaviors. Many were written by very accomplished riders or trainers. A few of the really outstanding books I've read over and over again and have learned something new each time. Nevertheless, it also has become apparent to me why many people eventually become disillusioned about the prospect of training horses.

First, not only are there seemingly endless numbers of things that a horse must be taught, but there are multiple methods for training each one. And, some methods even appear to be contradictory to others. How does a trainer choose among them? Or, after having chosen, how do you know that you are correctly implementing the method? How do you know whether the training is proceeding well or if the method should be abandoned and another tried? Should you stop now or should you continue? Are you asking too much too fast? Is the horse tired? Is he bored? Should you try to make him do it when he doesn't respond and, if not, then what? There can be one dilemma after another.

Second, even if a writer could anticipate all of the different ways that a horse might respond during training, it would be a formidable task to describe how to proceed under every possible permutation. Moreover, it would be prohibitive to read. I remember a time when I was watching an accomplished trainer teach a horse to "give to the bit." Suddenly, after a fair amount of time with little progress, the horse unexpectedly lay down on his side. He lay there totally unmoving for several minutes before the trainer encouraged the horse to get up. A short time later the horse lay down again. The trainer had anticipated the horse "giving to the bit" to relieve rein pressure. The horse found a different solution. Do you think step-by-step instructions would have anticipated this response from the horse? No way!

Admittedly, this is an exceptionally dramatic example of how horses can respond in unanticipated ways. Nevertheless, you can be certain that if you try to train solely by following a step-by-step formula, at some point, the horse will respond in a way that you did not expect. I guarantee it. There are far too many options that the horse can take to be anticipated. What then? I have a mental image of a computer that just crashed and the message reads "Frozen From Frustration."

The words of the Renaissance genius Leonardo da Vinci are particularly pertinent. He said, "Those who devote themselves to practice without science are like sailors who put to sea without rudder or compass and who can never be certain where they are going." The analogy holds true for training horses. If you attempt to train without fundamental principles to guide you, you are destined to find yourself adrift with no land in sight. On the other hand, if you have just a few basic rules at your command, you can navigate toward an enjoyable horse with relative ease.

Have you ever been impressed by a professional trainer who seemingly has a plan for teaching horses almost anything or for dealing with any behavioral problem that might arise? Do you think that trainer has total recall of step-by-step instructions for dealing with endless training goals? Of course not! Such people have a firm, often intuitive, understanding of a few fundamental principles, and they know how to use them effectively to address a variety of training objectives. You can do the same. It will broaden your training prowess and allow you to intelligently adapt as circumstances change.

In the chapters that follow, 10 fundamental principles for training horses are described. I think of them as *golden rules* that should be avidly adhered to during every interaction with a horse. The original golden rule says, "Do unto others as you would have them do unto you." Likewise, the golden rules of horse training are ethics of conduct. They define how an individual should act in order to produce a cooperative and stress-free horse.

In fact, the golden rules are the elements—the irreducible constituents—of every gentle and tactful training method. There are virtually an unlimited number of training methods, which can differ depending on the situation, inclinations of the trainer, style of riding, training objective, etc. Nevertheless, all effective training methods are based on a small number of fundamental principles. On the surface, different methods for addressing a training objective can appear quite dissimilar, even contradictory, but the underlying, fundamental principle often is the same. Just as the elements of the periodic table can be combined and recombined in endlessly different ways to create new substances, these elements of training can be applied in endless ways to create new training methods.

Some of the golden rules that are described in this book were known, or at least practiced, in one form or another by Xenophon and by horsemen who lived long before him, but they all have a firm foundation in modern learning or behavioral theory. Some are common sense; some are not. None are difficult to comprehend, but skill and finesse facilitate their implementation.

The discussion in this book is targeted for improving the performance of horses that have already had some training and can be ridden, but the golden rules apply to every stage of training from the most basic up to "High School" dressage as practiced at the famed Spanish Riding School of Vienna. They also are pertinent to every style of riding— horses learn according to the same laws regardless of whether they are ridden Western, English, Spanish, French, German, etc. In addition, the golden rules that apply to riding also apply to handling horses from the ground, although the methods of application can be quite different under the two circumstances.

The golden rules are discussed within a context of four general areas that together form the infrastructure for a pleasant and responsive horse. In short, a horse, regardless of the riding discipline, should be optimally sensitive and responsive to aids and cues (Chapter II), he should not do things that are disagreeable when handled from the ground or under saddle (Chapters III and IV), and he should not be fearful of his surroundings (Chapters V and VI). However, don't be intimidated by the apparent breadth of the topics. As you will see, there is a consistency in the fundamental principles for addressing these different training objectives. The golden rules for optimizing responsiveness to signals described in Chapter II are of paramount importance. They are the keystones for effective communication with a horse and the lifeblood of every effective training method.

CHAPTER

IMPROVING SENSITIVITY TO AIDS AND CUES

Transitions are Synonymous With Training

Training is sometimes envisioned as something that happens only during the early years of a horse's life or during special sessions that are separate from normal handling and riding. That is a misconception. Each time you ask a horse to change something that he is doing, that is, ask for a transition, whether from the ground or saddle, you are training. There are no exceptions. It doesn't matter whether the horse is "green" or a seasoned veteran. It makes no difference whether you are signaling for a newly learned response or one that the horse has made thousands of times. *Every time you ask a horse to do anything, he is learning one thing or another whether it is your intention or not.* Transitions are synonymous with training. Each one is comprised of a signal, a response and a reward—three crucial components of every training paradigm. In the most elementary terms, all training breaks down to teaching a horse to do something (the response) when asked (the signal). In theory, it's as simple as that.

In practice, there's a little more to it. For each of the three components of a transition—that is, the signal, the response and the reward—there are golden rules that define a rider's (or handler's) role and responsibilities. Obedience and performance progressively improve only when those rules are adhered to steadfastly and applied with competency.

In this chapter, I describe how these golden rules can be applied to improve sensitivity and responsiveness to aids and cues. However, as you will see as the following chapters unfold, these same rules are the *sine qua non*—essential elements—of virtually all tactful training. Even the golden rules for desensitizing horses to their surroundings are derivatives of those for sensitizing horses to aids and cues (see Chapters V and VI). You might also be surprised to find out that even horses adhere to these same golden rules for optimizing sensitivity to signals when communicating with one another (See Chapter IV).

The Signal

Signal for Transitions, Not to Maintain the Status Quo

Different people have different meanings for the terms "aid" and "cue." Some reserve the term "aid" for English-style riding and "cue" for Western-style riding. Others use the terms interchangeably. If I were pressed for my definitions, I would define "cue" as any sign that is designed to elicit a particular response from a horse. An aid, to me, is a special type of cue—

one that is meant to modify the movement or balance of a horse under saddle. Nevertheless, it is a rather esoteric distinction with no real practical value. Aids and cues, regardless of how the terms are used, are simply signals that are intended to elicit a specific response from a horse. *They are directives that tell a horse to change something that he is doing.* The first golden rule is the quintessence of this concept.

GOLDEN RULE #1

Aids and Cues are Signals for Change

The second golden rule is a logical consequence of the first: If aids and cues tell a horse to do something different, then, it follows that they should not be given when a horse is already doing what is desired. Would you tell another person to do something if they were already doing it? Not usually, I'm sure. It wouldn't serve any purpose and it might even irritate the other individual. That means that signals should always be terminated as soon as the horse begins to do what has been asked of him. They should not be used to maintain the status quo.

GOLDEN RULE #2

Signals Should Stop as Soon as the Horse Begins to Make an Acceptable Response

When riding, a signal should cause a prompt transformation in the horse's gait, speed, direction or balance. When it does, the rider should stop signaling immediately. The cessation of the signal does not have to be a dramatic, overt event; in a well-trained horse it can be so subtle that it is invisible to onlookers. Nevertheless, even though it might require only the slightest action from the rider, the horse must recognize the cessation of the signal as a total return to "neutral."

Ideally, the horse's response to an aid should itself terminate the signal. It should feel to the rider as if the horse moved away from the aid, releasing pressure. Then, the rider should harmonize with the horse by staying balanced and maintaining a body position that conforms to that of the horse and his movement. The aids should remain silent until the next transition. If constant pressure is maintained with the reins or legs while a horse is doing what he has been asked to do, he will become insensitive to the aids as a result of a phenomenon known as "sensory adaptation."

Normally, sensory adaptation functions to enhance an individual's ability to cope effectively with his surroundings. I am certain that you have experienced it firsthand many times. For example, you undoubtedly are familiar with the process of "dark adaptation," such as when you turn the lights off before going to bed. At first, it is difficult to see; then, as time passes, the surroundings gradually become more visible. There are significant physiological changes that take place as this happens: Almost immediately, the pupil of the eye enlarges to allow more light to enter and stimulate the retina. Then, chemical changes take place within the rods and cones of the retina to make it more likely that light-sensitive molecules will be struck by photons. Cones become fully dark-adapted within about 5–10 minutes as a result of the chemical changes and rods are completely dark adapted after about 20–30 minutes.

All of the senses, with the possible exception of the sense of pain, are capable of such physiological adaptations. But sensory adaptations do not usually result in enhanced sensitivity as in dark adaptation. More often, the adaptation is one of desensitization. For example, do you remember the first time that you wore a ring on your finger? At first, it probably felt like a huge bulge around your finger, but after a while you more than likely didn't even notice that it was there. The same thing probably happened as you became accustomed to wearing a watch or some other article of jewelry or clothing. Such adaptations to constant pressure occur rapidly and are associated with a decrease in the frequency of firing of the sensory neurons that transmit information from peripheral tissues, like the skin and muscles, to the central nervous system.

Desensitization normally plays an important adaptive role. It minimizes distractions from things in the surroundings that are unchanging and insignificant to the survival or well being of the individual, thereby allowing more attention to be given to things that are more significant. However, this same adaptive process works against riders who maintain constant rein or leg pressure. Then, physiological changes take place that make the bit and the rider's legs less noticeable to the horse. Consequently, stronger signals are required to elicit responses. Then, the horse gets branded as "hard-mouthed" and "dead-sided."

Nevertheless, I do not want to give you the impression that the insensitivity is irreversible because it involves physiological changes. That isn't so. Just as dark adaptation reverses when you return to a brighter environment, the deadening effect of constant pressure reverses as rein and leg pressure are consistently released when the horse begins to make acceptable responses to signals.

In the beginning, the horse might slow down when leg pressure is released and speed up or change directions when rein contact is relaxed. If he does, signal again to restore the desired speed or direction. Then, stop signaling. Be persistent. Repeat the sequence as often as necessary. In so doing, horses eventually learn to maintain the specified speed and direction on their own, without effort from the rider.

You can facilitate the learning process if you stay alert for the slightest changes that are initiated by the horse rather than by you. As soon as you detect them, signal and restore the speed or direction that you desire. The earlier you detect and correct deviations, the faster the horse will learn to maintain the status quo until you signal for a change. The subject of "corrections" is discussed in more detail in Chapter V.

Don't Take "No" for an Answer

Aids and cues tell a horse to change something that he is doing. The horse should respond promptly to the signal. If he does not, the rider (or handler) should continue to signal until he makes an acceptable response. *Horses should never be allowed to ignore a signal.* It doesn't matter whether the horse is being ridden indoors or outdoors or being handled in a stall, paddock or arena: aids and cues should be thought of as obligatory directives, not requests. That does not mean that they must be forceful. A signal can be a directive regardless of its strength. One that is so subtle that it is invisible to onlookers is still a directive that should be acknowledged.

G O L D E N   R U L E   # 3

Signals Should Never Be Ignored

In the beginning, horses do not typically respond to subtle signals. Nevertheless, it is important that they are always given an opportunity to do so. If a horse does not respond to the subtle signal, it should be made more emphatic. Its potency should be increased in steps, without being harsh or ruthless, until he makes an acceptable response.

When a signal terminates before a horse responds, it tends to make him less sensitive to the signal. This is a serious error that is not uncommon. I can't tell you how many times I have watched individuals stop in the middle of trying to elicit a response from a horse only to make some casual comment to a bystander or to go do something else. I cannot overemphasize the negative impact such actions have on a horse's responsiveness. If it is reasonable to signal for a response (see the discussion on page 38 in the section titled "The Response"), do not stop signaling until the horse makes it. Find some way to elicit the response or, at least, some approximation of it. Any interruption of more than a couple of seconds makes it that much harder to elicit the response on the next try, and, in the long run, it completely deadens the horse to the signal.

It is very important, however, to give a horse time to respond before making a signal more emphatic. Be fair, give him a second or so to respond, but don't delay too long. There is a fine line between allowing a horse time to respond and allowing him to ignore the signal. The difference should be readily recognizable to anyone who is adept at reading the body language of horses. If you haven't reached that level of competency yet, as a general rule, don't wait any longer than two seconds before increasing the potency of a signal.

Increasing Signal Potency

In some instances, a signal can be made more emphatic simply by increasing its strength. However, this is true only if the signal has an intrinsic ability to evoke the desired response. Rein aids fall into this category. If a horse does not respond to a light rein signal, its potency can be increased by intensifying rein pressure.

Often, however, aids and cues have little intrinsic ability to evoke the desired response. Their potency is largely derived from training. In those cases, increasing the strength of the signal has little impact on its potency. Voice cues are a good example; they have little inherent power beyond getting a horse's attention. If a horse doesn't understand the word "whoa," it will do little good to shout it. It is much more effective to repeat the word "whoa" followed a fraction of a second later by what I call a supporting signal, like pressure on the reins, to which the horse has a natural inclination to slow and stop. *Supporting signals must always have an inherent tendency to evoke the desired response.*

The primary and supporting signals should continue to be given in tandem until the horse makes an acceptable response. As a general rule, the supporting signal should be given half a second to two seconds after the onset of the primary signal. The intensity of the primary signal should remain unchanged while that of the supporting signal increases until the response is evoked. With repeated and persistent pairing of the primary and supporting signals, the horse will eventually learn to respond to the primary signal alone. For those interested in theory, this type of training is called "classical conditioning," the type discovered by Ivan Pavlov. What I refer to as the primary signal, Pavlov called the "condition stimulus," and the supporting signal is what Pavlov called the "unconditioned stimulus." It is a very powerful training paradigm when applied correctly.

Leg aids, like voice cues, also have little inherent power. That is, they do not naturally make horses go forward or faster. At the beginning of training, many horses either do not respond to leg pressure, or they might even go backward. Thus, if a horse does not respond to a leg aid, there is no reason to increase pressure or to spur him. Contrary to popular belief, spurs are not a natural forward driving aid. Instead, spurs tend to cause horses to tuck their croup downward and step farther under their body with their hind legs. Think about how you would respond to sharp pressure on both sides of your body. More than likely your stomach muscles would tighten, shortening your front and rounding your back. Horses naturally respond the same way. Consequently, at advanced levels of riding, spurs can be used to facilitate collection and improve lightness. Individuals who do not possess the skill and understanding necessary for implementing these advanced concepts certainly should not wear them. Even then, I question their value except in the hands of the most skilled riders seeking exceptional levels of performance.

If a horse does not respond to light leg pressure, the best strategy is to continue to signal with light pressure accompanied by a tap on the hindquarters with a whip or crop a second or so later. Tap progressively harder until the horse responds. Horses have a natural inclination to respond to a tap on the hindquarters by moving forward faster. As soon as the horse makes an acceptable response, release the leg pressure and stop tapping with the whip. With repetition, horses learn to move forward promptly to light leg pressure alone.

Of course, I realize that few people carry a whip all of the time, and we probably all have made horses go forward or faster by increasing leg pressure or by kicking or spurring them. These methods usually do work on horses that have a reasonable understanding of what leg pressure means, but for one reason or another are being disobedient, perhaps because they are distracted or fearful of something in front of them. However, if you must always resort to these methods, then the horse should be retrained to respond to light leg pressure using a whip and the method described in the preceding paragraph.

For those occasional situations when a well-trained horse fails to respond to light pressure and you are not carrying a whip, it is much more effective to bump with the calf of your leg than to squeeze harder with your legs. I usually bump in sets of three ... bump, bump, bump ... which seems natural to me and is easily detected by the horse.

Discontinuous signals are always more noticeable than steady signals and therefore are more likely to elicit a reaction from a horse that is distracted or being disobedient for some other reason. Also, riders often become stiff when applying steady leg pressure making it more difficult for them to follow the movement of the horse. After I bump, I give the horse a brief moment to respond. If he doesn't, I repeat the sequence bumping a little harder. If he still does not respond, I follow the same sequence but bump with my heel. I never stop signaling until the horse makes an acceptable response—if I have to reach around and slap the horse on his rump with my hand, so be it.

Sometimes I see riders lunging forward and backward in the saddle while kicking in an attempt to make their horses go forward faster. Apparently, they believe that the momentum from their forward thrust encourages the horse to go faster. Sometimes it works; the forward thrust of the rider's weight throws the horse onto his forehand and consequently he speeds up in an attempt to keep his balance. Even so, it usually is totally ineffective, and it is certainly an unsightly method that should be avoided.

If the Horse is Unlikely to Respond Satisfactorily, Don't Signal

Occasionally, you might encounter circumstances under which a horse is not likely to respond regardless of how persistently you signal. If you encounter such situations, don't signal. This is likely to happen most often when horses are unrestrained or when they are frightened or excited. For example, it is useless to say "whoa" to a horse that is running free and doesn't want to be caught. It only confirms to him that he can ignore the voice command to stop. Likewise, it can be unreasonable to ask for certain responses from horses that are excited or frightened. There is no way that such horses are going to stand still, for instance, unless you resort to force or violence.

In the words of Brig. Gen. Kurt Albrecht, a former commander of the Spanish Riding School of Vienna, "The horse must always be in the proper psychological conditions before any of the physical aids can produce its intended effects."[7] *It is much better to focus on improving a horse's mental state when he is frightened or excited than to give him commands that might only exacerbate the situation by escalating his emotional state even further* (see Chapters III and IV). Such situations, however, should become rare as the horse's training progresses and he becomes more experienced. Over the long run, proper training makes horses less fearful and less excitable.

"Speak" Clearly

If you have poor grammar and mumble, even a highly educated individual will have difficulty deciphering your messages. The same is true for aids and cues. Rules 1–3, as described above, are cornerstones of training. But, when applying those rules, remember that each signal should be distinct and readily distinguishable; otherwise, the impact of the message will be compromised. If your "grammar and speech" are poor, it will be difficult for the horse to recognize and interpret your signals.

Signals Should Be Distinct

Riding skill, obviously, is a chief factor that affects the ability to signal clearly. A horse can much more readily detect a signal from a rider with quiet hands and legs than from one who bounces in the saddle and has hands and legs that wobble about. But it is not unusual to see even an experienced rider do things that make it more difficult for a horse to respond to a signal. It is rather common, for example, to see riders lean forward when asking a horse to slow or stop, or to lean one way while asking him to move sideways in the other direction. In both cases, the rider's weight works against the horse, making it more difficult for him to comply with the signal.

Have you ever carried someone on you shoulders or had someone carry you on their shoulders in a swimming pool? If you haven't, try it. You will find that it is natural for the person on the bottom to shift his or her position to keep the person on top balanced above them. If the person on the top leans forward a bit, the one on the bottom will quickly move forward to rebalance the load. Likewise, if the person on the top leans toward the left, the one on the bottom will move left to recenter the load. The same holds true regardless of the direction; the person on the bottom always follows the center of gravity of the one on the top. The same is true for horses. Weight aids have an intrinsic ability to evoke the correct response when applied properly. *If you want a horse to move in a certain direction, shift your weight that way and the horse will naturally follow.* Do not lean in the opposite direction in an attempt to "push" the horse in the direction that you want him to go.

Hand Without Legs, Legs Without Hand

Another mistake riders sometimes make is to signal with conflicting aids simultaneously. More than 100 years ago, the French riding master François Baucher extolled the use of "hand without legs, legs without hand."[8] He was advocating the use of only one aid at a time for transitions in speed, gait or direction. This might not be an entirely attainable goal, particularly with regard to advanced levels of riding. Then, an artistic interplay between fine aids is often necessary to delicately sculpt a horse's movement. Sometimes even a momentary cooperation between opposing aids is necessary for rebalancing or bending the horse or for initiating certain lateral movements. Nevertheless, the simultaneous application of opposing aids should certainly be avoided in the beginning stages of training and also thereafter, except under advanced circumstances. There is absolutely no question that opposing signals diminish the sensitivity of a horse. Ask a horse to go forward while restraining with the reins and you will erase the conditioning that endows the legs with the power to produce impulsion. You will create a "dead-sided" horse that is also likely to be heavy in your hands.

Knowing When to Signal

Riders often signal for transitions between and within gaits at less-than-optimal points during a horse's stride.

Consequently, the horse is either slow to respond to the aid or he hurriedly shuffles his feet in an attempt to comply with the signal. A good rule of thumb to keep in mind is that *a foot or a leg that is in the air is already committed to a certain flight path; its trajectory can only be changed by unbalancing the horse* which, obviously, is undesirable. Therefore, if you want to influence the action of a certain leg, in theory the signal should be given just before the foot leaves the ground. In practice, however, it is usually necessary to signal a slight bit earlier so that the horse has time to process the signal before the foot leaves the ground.

Some riders instinctively signal at the appropriate time during the stride, others do not. If you are among the latter, with repetition and practice you might gain a natural feel for when to signal. But, if you have been struggling for some time without significant improvement, you might have to take a more analytical approach.

In particular, it might be helpful to learn the sequence of footfalls at the different gaits. This is merely a matter of memorization. The sequence for walk, trot and canter are as follows:

WALK. In the walk, the horse moves his feet one after another producing a four-beat gait. The horse always has two or three feet on the ground. Consequently, there is no period of suspension as in the trot and canter. When going from halt to walk, horses naturally move a front foot first. As you will see in Chapter IV, this is an important characteristic of the halt-to-walk transition. Nevertheless, because the power for the walk comes from the hind feet, it is traditional to list the sequence of the footfalls beginning with a back foot. For example:

- Left hind
- Left fore
- Right hind
- Right fore

Sequence of footfalls at the walk.

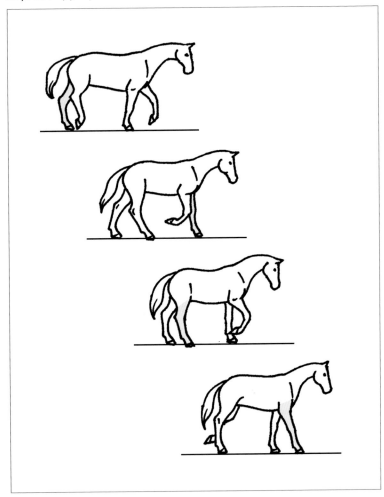

TROT. When a horse trots, he moves his right fore and left hind in unison and his left fore and right hind in unison. The pairs of legs that move together are called diagonals and are named according to the front foot: the right diagonal is the right fore and left hind, and the left diagonal is the left fore and right hind.

Sequence of footfalls at the trot.

The trot is conventionally described as a two-beat gait with each diagonal making a beat. However, in a true trot, following the movement of each diagonal there is a period when all four feet are off of the ground. This period of "suspension" is approximately equal to the period during which a diagonal pair of legs is on the ground. Thus, the trot is more accurately described as a four beat gait with two of the beats inaudible:

- Right fore, left hind

- Period of suspension

- Left fore, right hind

- Period of suspension

It is during the period of suspension that horses execute responses to aids. That means that an aid that signals for a response while the relevant foot is on the ground (see above) must be released during the period of suspension for optimal compliance with Golden Rule #2 (Signals should stop as soon as the horse begins to make an acceptable response). The release of the aid serves two important purposes: First, it allows the horse the unimpeded freedom to complete the requested response and, second, as elaborated below, it rewards the horse for making the desired response.

When there is no period of suspension between the diagonals, it is not a true trot; it is more accurately categorized as a diagonalized walk. The western "jog trot" is an example of a diagonalized walk; the horse moves his legs in diagonal pairs but there is no period of suspension during the stride. This makes the jog trot comparatively easy to sit. Horses should also move backward by alternately moving the diagonal pairs of legs without a period of suspension. If the diagonal legs do not move in unison, the gait is faulty probably due to a contracted (i.e., hollow), rather than stretched (i.e., rounded), topline.

   CANTER: The canter is conventionally described as a three-beat gait with a period of suspension between

Sequence of footfalls for a left lead canter.

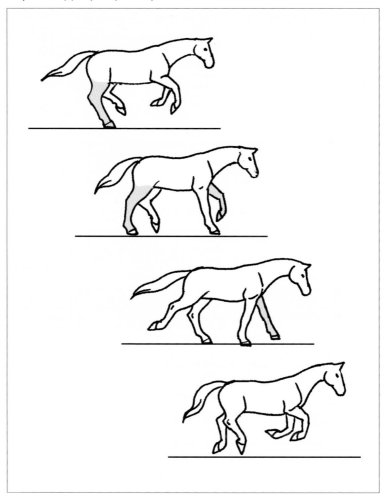

strides. It is an asymmetrical gait in that the fore- and hind legs on one side "lead" the fore- and hind leg on the other side. A canter stride is described according to the leading leg and, therefore, there is a left lead and a right lead canter. Horses naturally strike off into a canter by stepping up and pushing off with the hind leg on the side opposite to the leading leg. The second beat of the stride is made by a diagonal pair of legs. The third beat is made by the leading foreleg which is followed by a period of suspension. Here is the sequence for the right and left lead canters:

Left lead canter:

- Right hind
- Right fore, left hind (i.e., right diagonal)
- Left fore
- Period of suspension

Right lead canter:

- Left hind
- Left fore, right hind (i.e., left diagonal)
- Right fore
- Period of suspension

Feeling When to Signal

If you have trouble feeling what your horse's feet are doing, there are a number of things you might try to focus on. At the walk and trot, as a hind leg moves forward, the rider's seat bone on that same side also moves forward. Conversely, as the hind leg moves backward on the ground, the rider's seat

bone on that side moves backward. That means that the
optimal time to influence the movement of a hind leg is during the time when the rider's seat bone on that same side is
moving backward. For example, horses naturally strike off on
a right lead canter by stepping up and pushing off on their

Sequence of footfalls for a right lead canter.

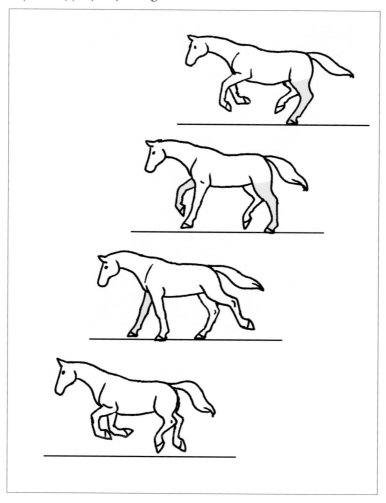

left hind leg. Therefore, the optimal time to signal for a right lead canter is while the left hind foot is on the ground—that is, when the rider's left seat bone is moving backward. Conversely, the best time to signal for a left lead canter is while the right hind foot is on the ground; that is, when the rider's right seat bone is moving backward. Obviously, to detect such subtle movements, a rider must be extremely well seated, with seat bones that are "plugged in" to the movement of the horse.

Alternatively, you might try paying attention to the horse's rib cage and belly; try to feel the side-to-side move-

As a horse walks and trots, his center of gravity shifts toward the hind leg that is on the ground. The horse in the drawing is walking. Notice that his right hind foot is on the ground and his midsection is displaced toward that side.

ment. As a horse's hind foot moves forward at the walk and trot, his midsection shifts toward the other side. This provides room for the forward swing of the leg and puts the horse's weight more toward the hind foot that is on the ground. It is an easy relationship to remember because your midsection does the same thing as you walk, although not nearly so noticeably. Better yet, try standing still and lifting up one of your feet by bending the leg at the knee and hip. Notice how your midsection naturally hollows a little on the side where you lift your leg and bulges out a bit on the opposite side. As a horse walks and trots, his midsection is likewise displaced toward the side where his hind foot is on the ground. That means that the optimal time to influence a hind leg is when the horse's midsection is shifted to that side. For example, the best time to signal for a right lead canter is when the horse's midsection is shifted to the left.

At first, you might also want to watch the movement of the horse's shoulders, but, ultimately, it is much better for a rider to feel the correct time to signal rather than to watch for it. In any event, if you know the sequence of the footfalls in a gait, you can tell what each foot is doing at any given moment by watching the movement of the horse's shoulders. The shoulder moves forward and backward along with the leg. The trot, as described above, is a diagonal gait. The right fore and left hind legs move together, and the left fore and right hind legs move together. That means that the right shoulder moves along with the left hind, and the right shoulder moves along with the left hind. The optimal time to influence a hind leg, therefore, is when the shoulder on the opposite side is moving backward. For example, the best time to signal for a right lead canter from the trot is when the horse's right shoulder is moving backward—that is, when the left hind foot is on the ground.

You also can ask a friend or instructor to help you learn to feel the correct time to signal for transitions. Have them call out the word "now" each time the foot you want to influence is about to leave the ground. Then, try calling out "now" yourself and let the other person see if your timing is correct. With practice, you will develop a better feeling for when to ask for the desired response and, eventually, the timing will become second nature to you.

The Response

Decisions, Decisions

The response is the horse's responsibility. The rider (or handler) gives a signal and the horse responds. The rider's role in this case is solely judgmental. There are two decisions that must be made. The first one should be made even before the signal is given. That is, is it reasonable to ask for the response? If not, then the signal should not be given. If a rider asks for a response that a horse is not capable of making, he will become insensitive to the signal. It violates Golden Rule #3 (Signals should never be ignored). In this case, the horse isn't actually "ignoring" the signal, but in practice, the difference is inconsequential—the signal is given and no response follows. In addition, if a rider persists in asking for a response that a horse cannot make, there is a good chance that it will lead to the development of unwanted behaviors. If the horse cannot comply with a signal, he'll find another way to free himself from the rider's persistent demand. And it is not likely to be by doing something that is considered pleasant. Many times bad behavior is unfortunately ascribed to a fractious nature when, in truth, it is the result of unreasonable demands.

The second decision is whether or not a response was acceptable. That is, did the horse do what he was asked to do? This is a crucial issue because it will determine whether or not the horse is rewarded or whether the person will continue to ask for the response.

Make It Easy

Both decisions that must be made regarding a response are subjective. There are no hard and fast guidelines for making them. It is a case where there is no substitute for experience. It is part of what makes training an art as well as a science. Nevertheless, there is one golden rule that should not be violated when making these decisions:

GOLDEN RULE #5

A Response Should Be Easy for the Horse to Make

I can think of only one instance where it might be necessary to ask for more than a horse can give easily. That would be in the conditioning of a horse. Then, it is usually necessary to urge a horse toward the limits of his capacities, whether to increase his strength, stamina or suppleness. Even here, however, there is a fine line between the amount of work required to improve a horse and the amount that leads to physical and mental deterioration. In all other instances, a person should ask only for what a horse can do easily. It is the only way to maintain tact and gentleness in training. *If you ask a horse to do something that, for one reason or another, is difficult for him to do, you will undoubtedly have to be forceful to get him to do it.*

This does not mean that you can never teach a horse to do anything that is difficult. The process of training itself should make what was initially mentally or physically difficult for the horse, easy. It might be helpful to think of training as a ladder. Each step that is taken makes the next one easier to reach. The trick is to identify the steps that will eventually lead to your ultimate goal.

When training a horse to do something new, be satisfied with the slightest hint of the response you are seeking. For example, when training a horse to back up, at first, don't ask for any more than a mere shift in the horse's weight toward his hindquarters. As that becomes easy to elicit, ask for a little more. Improve the response in small increments. Continue the process until the horse responds easily with the full desired response—in the example, a full step backward.

If at any point along the progression you encounter resistance, increase the potency of the signal until the horse makes the response (Golden Rule #2: Signals should never be ignored). However, it is important that the horse remains calm and relaxed throughout the process. Do not jeopardize that prerequisite by being overly rigid about what constitutes an acceptable response. Sometimes it is necessary to accept less than you might have already achieved. Don't hesitate to take a step back in the training sequence or even to start over. Go slowly. Build on success. Training should never be taxing or oppressive to a horse.

Don't Practice to Failure

Once you can elicit a desired response, don't wear it out. It is common to see people continue to ask for a response until the horse fails to make it. Sometimes with repetition horses simply become confused, uncertain that the response is correct, and they try something else. They also can become fatigued or unbalanced with repetition. I see this problem often when horses are being taught to back or move sideways or to go on the bit. Initially, maybe the horse takes one or two good steps backward or laterally, or stays on the bit for a period of time easily. Then as the trainer's demands become more ambitious, the horse becomes unbalanced and fatigued to a point where he can no longer comply. Practicing outlasts the horse's ability to respond correctly. I call this "practicing to failure." Then, convinced that the horse "knows" the correct response, the trainer concludes that the failure to make it is due to some personality flaw and the resolve to elicit it becomes irrational and forceful.

It is far better to "practice to success." That is, stop while the response is fresh. Quality is more important than quantity. There is no harm in practicing, but give the horse frequent intervals for rest and relaxation. And, always make sure that you end on a positive note. Tomorrow is another day. If the horse remains calm and relaxed during training, his responsiveness will improve overnight, sometimes quite dramatically. It is then, especially during periods of sleep, that the memory consolidation takes place that is crucial for the acquisition of new skills.

Expect Regressions in Performance

Finally, even if a response is easy for a horse, it doesn't mean that he will make it readily all of the time and under every circumstance. In fact, you should expect horses to regress occasionally, especially when conditions change or when they are presented with situations that frighten or excite them. For example, a horse that readily goes forward to light leg pressure in an arena might not do so when he encounters a water crossing on his first trail ride. Likewise, a horse that leads well might not step right up into a trailer the first time that he is asked. But even minor changes can affect responsiveness. Horses are much more sensitive and reactive to changes in their surroundings than we are.

It is important that the rider (or handler) does not make the mistake of concluding that such regressions in responsiveness are a sign of an intractable nature. If you have been involved with horses for any length of time, I'm sure you've heard someone who's having trouble with a horse say out of exasperation something like, "He knows how to do this. He does it all the time at home." Maybe so, but, that isn't a guarantee that he will do it readily when he is at a show or on the trail or even under every condition when asked at home.

Don't become frustrated; such occurrences are natural and important phases of training. In the words of James Fillis (1834–1913), who was considered one of the greatest riders of his time, "Sooner or later, in the course of training, disagreement between rider and horse is going to occur; we cannot be certain of a horse's submissiveness [i.e., responsiveness to the aids[9]] if we never give orders that it would rather not obey."[10] Therefore, when you run into situations where your horse is not as responsive as you would like, consider it an opportunity to train him even further. Over time and with exposure to a variety of situations his responsiveness will become more and more reliable.

The Reward

Reward Promptly

It is a mistake to think of a reward as something that benefits the horse alone. A reward is not just a favor that is graciously given while expecting nothing in return. Quite the contrary! If you reward a horse effectively and consistently for behaving correctly, you will be the beneficiary of a horse that is sensitive to your signals and that will respond enthusiastically with a cooperative attitude. If, on the other hand, you fail to reward a horse, his sensitivity and responsiveness will dwindle and you will suffer the consequences of a less-than-willing disposition. More than 50 years ago the brilliant rider and trainer Capt. Marcel Beudant captured the essence of training in one simple phrase: "Ask for much, be content with little, and reward often."[11]

An effective reward strengthens the association—or what learning theorists call "the bond"—between the signal and the correct response. As the bond becomes stronger, the horse makes the response to the signal more readily: He becomes more sensitive to the signal and his first response is more likely to be an acceptable one. A number of factors can influence how effective a reward is in this regard, but one is of paramount importance for training horses:

GOLDEN RULE #6

Rewards Enhance Sensitivity to Signals Only when They Immediately Follow an Acceptable Response

The effectiveness of a reward declines rapidly with time after a response is made. Therefore, it is imperative that a horse is rewarded immediately, within a spit second if possible, after he makes an acceptable response. If three or four seconds elapse, it's too late. Oh sure, the horse might still enjoy the reward, and it might improve his disposition, but it will contribute little toward maintaining or improving the desired response.

Positive and Negative Rewards

When riding, the primary reward for an acceptable response is the release of the aid that signaled for the response, that is, a reduction in rein or leg pressure or a rebalancing of the rider's center of gravity over that of the horse. In the early phase of training, rein and leg aids or their supporting signals only evoke a response when they are sufficiently emphatic to bother the horse. Remember the guideline discussed under Golden Rule #3: "If the horse does not respond to the subtle signal, ... its potency should be increased in steps ... until he makes an acceptable response." As a rider does so, the signal becomes annoying to the horse and he looks for a way to terminate it. The annoyance is the incentive that induces the horse to action. It is what motivates him to respond to the aid. When he does, the rider should stop signaling *immediately*. Sound familiar? It should! It was repeatedly emphasized under Golden Rule #2 (Signals should stop as soon as the horse begins to make an acceptable response). The release of the aid rewards the horse by terminating the annoyance.

As the training progresses and the horse becomes more sensitive and responsive to an aid, a transition occurs. He no longer responds to eliminate the annoyance caused by the signal. Instead, he responds to avoid it. That is, he learns to respond before the potency of the signal increases to a point where it is bothersome—provided, of course, that you give him the opportunity to do so. Remember my admonition: "In the beginning, horses do not typically respond to subtle signals. Nevertheless, it is important that they are always given an opportunity to do so." If you don't provide that opportunity, the horse will never learn that he can avoid, rather than escape, the annoyance caused by the signal. Consequently, he will never learn to respond to a refined aid.

More often than not, signals for controlling horses from the ground also become annoying as their potency is increased. The termination of the signal is, again, the primary reward for an acceptable response. For example, many people teach their horse to lift a foot by pinching the tendon on the back of the lower leg; farriers typically use this method. When the horse does not respond to a light pinch, they increase the pressure until the horse lifts his foot. The reward for lifting the foot is the termination of the pressure on the tendon.

Technically, when you take away or terminate something that a horse dislikes, such as an annoyance or a stimulus that causes discomfort, after he makes an acceptable response, it is called a negative reinforcer or, in lay terms, negative reward. When a rider (or handler) stops signaling, it is a negative reward. It is of paramount importance for increasing the sensitivity of horses to aids and cues. Nevertheless, don't jump to the conclusion that there is no reason to ever do anything positive for a horse. That is certainly far from true. Positive rewards can also contribute to optimizing sensitivity and responsiveness, and they have extremely beneficial effects on a horse's enthusiasm. They can be given as you stop signaling or immediately thereafter. They cannot be a substitute for the termination of the signal. That must occur every single time that a horse makes an acceptable response—100 percent of the time; no exceptions.

Treats are a good example of a positive reward. However, some individuals are hesitant to use treats in training because horses can become nippy if they are repeatedly hand fed. This is a legitimate concern. Nevertheless, I happen to enjoy feeding treats to my horses, and it clearly increases their enthusiasm for cooperating with my wishes. I simply insist on good "table manners." They must stand quietly and behave politely to get a treat. I never give a treat to a horse while he is nibbling or nuzzling my clothing or me.

He may never "ask" for the treat. But, it is not imperative that you use treats when training horses. There are plenty of other things that horses enjoy.

A gentle stroke or soft rub also can be naturally rewarding to horses. A slap on the side of the neck is not enjoyable to horses even though it is common to see riders do so when they are pleased by a horse's performance. If you slap a horse that has not been desensitized to such treatment, I can assure you that the reaction you will get from the horse will not be one of joyfulness; more than likely, he will flinch, jump or run away in an attempt to escape or avoid another blow. Have you ever had a friend or relative who would slap you on the back as a sign of "affection" or approval? I have, and I didn't like it much. I don't think horses like being slapped either. Even when horses have been desensitized to a slap and no longer react to it, I suspect that they still do not like it—they have simply learned to stoically endure it. It is far better to gently stroke or softly rub them.

A word or sound can also be rewarding to horses. Some soft tones and sounds are inherently pleasing to horses. For the most part, however, words and sounds are rewarding largely as a result of conditioning. If you repeatedly follow a word or sound with something that the horse naturally enjoys, such as a treat, it will become a signal that a reward is imminent. With repetition, the word or sound itself will become rewarding to a degree. This is the basis of so-called "clicker" training which has grown in popularity in recent years. Such rewards are very useful when it is inconvenient to use other types of positive rewards, such as while you are riding. I ride a Morgan stallion named Gabriel whose attitude is very positively affected by the words "good boy." In the early stages of his training, "good boy" was always followed by a piece of carrot. Now, I maintain the effectiveness of the words by following them from time to time with a treat, a gentle rub on the neck, a rest period and/or an opportunity to graze.

In the early stages of training a new behavior, horses should be lavishly rewarded immediately after every acceptable response: Stop signaling and simultaneously tell him he's a good boy. Then, pet him, give him a treat or let him graze or rest. Let him know you were pleased by what he did. But as the training progresses, positive rewards, in contrast to the

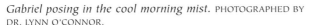

Gabriel posing in the cool morning mist. PHOTOGRAPHED BY DR. LYNN O'CONNOR.

termination of the signal, do not have to follow every acceptable response. In fact, it is better if they do not.

When positive rewards are given too liberally, they
lose their effectiveness through a process known as satiation.
It is a case where there can be too much of a good thing.
Positive rewards are only effective when they reduce a need,
like an appetite or desire. Scientists would say that there is a
positive correlation between the potency of a reward and the
magnitude of the need it fulfills. The greater the need, the better the reward. On the other hand, as the need becomes satiated, that is, satisfied, the reward naturally loses potency. This
relationship is perhaps easiest to understand for treats; they
are most effective as a reward when a horse is hungry or when
he hasn't had a treat for a while. Think of some treat that you
like. Take an ice cream sundae, for example. I bet a sundae
sounds better to you when you're hungry or when you haven't
had one for a while, right? Of course! And if you ate two sun-
daes in a row, it isn't likely that you will be too thrilled to get
a third one. Horses are no different. And, the relationship
between the magnitude of a need and the potency of a reward
holds true for every type of positive reward, not just treats. For
example, a period of rest is only positively rewarding if the
horse is tired to some degree. I wouldn't say that positive
rewards should be given out sparingly, but they should not be
delved out indiscriminately either. Tell a horse that he is a
"good boy" too often and the words will lose their value as a
positive reward.

The most effective strategy is to give positive rewards
intermittently. Try to give them after the horse responds just
a little bit better than normal or a little bit better than he had

been responding that day, or when you feel that the horse has tried a little bit harder than normal. Use them to instill a positive work ethic and to encourage the horse to strive for a higher level of performance. But don't be too stingy with positive rewards; remember the words of Capt. Beudant: "Ask for much, be content with little, and reward often."

Summary

To optimize a horse's sensitivity and responsiveness to aids and cues, signal only when you want him to change something that he is doing. The signal should be discreet and initially subtle. If the horse doesn't respond to the subtle signal, increase its potency until he makes an acceptable response. When he does, stop signaling immediately and, when appropriate, reward him with something that he enjoys.

CHAPTER

PREVENTING
UNDESIRABLE BEHAVIOR
UNDER SADDLE

The First Line of Defense

The golden rules that are described in Chapter II for optimizing sensitivity to signals are the first line of defense against undesirable behavior. When a rider rigorously adheres to those rules, the horse becomes progressively more pleasant to ride. Not only does his sensitivity to aids increase, he also becomes less likely to do things that are disagreeable. More often than not, undesirable behavior can be traced to a faulty use of the aids stemming from some breach of one or more of the golden rules laid down in Chapter II. Author Mary Twelveponies put it this way: "It's the hardest pill for all of us would-be horsemen to swallow but it is absolutely true—if the horse is not responding properly, we are doing something wrong."[12]

If a horse requires a lot of leg pressure to make him go forward, doesn't back up, leans heavily on the bit, swishes his tail incessantly, needs a flash noseband or some other device to keep his mouth from gaping open or his head from going up, or the like, I can assure you that it is not due to an inherently cantankerous nature or to some genetic deficiency in sensitivity or conformation. It is much more likely to be the result either of too little training or of training that did not conform to the golden rules. Even more severe types of misbehavior are often rider-induced. Rearing is a good example. There are two types of errors that commonly elicit it.

Sometimes, rearing emerges from the persistent application of opposing aids, a violation of Golden Rule #4 (Signals should be distinct). Essentially, the rider traps the horse between driving and restraining aids and, in trying to find a way to escape the confinement, the horse rears. Riders also can elicit rearing by relentlessly asking a horse to do something that he cannot do easily; that is, by violating Golden Rule #5 (A response should be easy for the horse to make). In this case, the task usually isn't one that is physically difficult for the horse; typically, it's one that is psychologically formidable. In essence, the rider's will and that of the horse clash. For example, frightened horses sometimes rear when riders try to force them to stand still by keeping strong, constant pressure on the bit.

Likewise, many other types of undesirable behavior can be traced to some infraction against the golden rules described in Chapter II. Others stem from insufficient training according to those rules. The information in this chapter, therefore, should be regarded as supplemental to Chapter II. Hopefully, it will provide an even deeper insight into the origins of undesirable behavior and how to deal with it more effectively. However, if you anticipate finding a catalog of behaviors in this chapter, you will be somewhat disappointed. Although a number of specific behaviors are discussed as examples, I have made no attempt to address each of the myriad of disagreeable things that horses potentially do under saddle; that would be a formidable, in fact, impossible, task. Instead, two golden rules for preventing and eliminating undesirable behavior are described. If you understand and can implement those rules, you will be capable of effectively dealing with almost any disagreeable thing a horse might do under saddle.

Rewards and Undesirable Behavior

There Is Always a Motive Behind Action

Unless it stems from an illness or physical discomfort, undesirable behavior usually does not suddenly appear in full bloom. It typically begins with a minor offense that the rider dismisses because it seems insignificant. But, over time, the horse begins to do it more often, for longer periods of time, and/or more intensely. Often the evolution occurs so gradually that it isn't even noticed. Then, the behavior reaches a threshold level of severity and suddenly there is a conscious recognition that a problem exists. To the rider, it might seem as if the disagreeable behavior erupted from out of nowhere. I would bet that, at one time or another, you have heard riders with a surprised expression exclaim something like, "I can't believe *Lil' Seraph* did that. He's never done it before." Maybe he hasn't, but it's likely that he has been building toward it for some time. The rider just overlooked the germinal stages.

When an undesirable behavior worsens, you can be sure that it is being rewarded somehow. There is always a motive behind action. In the most basic terms, horses behave in undesirable ways for only one reason: to get a reward. It could be to obtain something enjoyable (positive reward) but in most cases horses behave in disagreeable ways to elude something unpleasant (negative reward). It might be to escape from a persistent signal for a response he can't make or to evade a real or imagined threat. In some cases, the horse is just trying to protect himself from physical discomfort caused by the rider or tack or by a physical inadequacy or injury. Ordinary undesirable behaviors like spontaneous changes in speed, body alignment, gait or balance are typically efforts to conserve energy.

GOLDEN RULE #7

Undesirable Behavior Worsens Only if It Is Rewarded

Accordingly, there are two key elements to successfully preventing the development of undesirable behaviors. First, it is imperative that you stay alert for changes in behavior. Sudden changes deserve special, immediate attention because they can be indications that a horse is suffering some physical difficulty. More gradual changes also should not be overlooked. If unchecked, they can sometimes develop into severe problems that are much more difficult to eliminate than to prevent.

The second key to preventing the development of undesirable behavior pertains to the reward. It is crucial that riders do not inadvertently reward undesirable behavior. Sound simple? It is, most of the time. Nevertheless, it is among the most basic mistakes that people make, and it literally encourages horses to behave badly.

One of the most commonly cited errors that riders make is to release rein pressure at inappropriate moments. As described in Chapter II, when rein pressure is released immediately following a correct response, it reinforces that response. That is, it increases the likelihood that the horse will again make the correct response the next time the rein signal is given. However, when rein pressure is released while the horse is doing something undesirable, like pulling on the reins, "acting-up," shaking his head, rearing, etc., it reinforces that behavior. Consequently, the horse will be more likely to behave in the same disagreeable way the next time he finds himself under similar circumstances.

Perhaps an even more common error is to allow horses to rest after they do something that is disagreeable. It is natural for riders to "give the horse a chance to calm down" after things have gone badly. Unfortunately, most of the time it only reinforces the bad behavior. Even a brief break in the action can be a powerful reward. But the most blatant mistake, of course, is to dismount and end a ride because things just aren't going well—maybe *"Lil' Seraph* wasn't in the mood today." It is sad to say perhaps, but one of the most powerful rewards that you can give a horse is to stop riding and get off his back. It is one reason why you should always end a riding session on a good note. If you end after the horse has behaved disagreeably, you increase the likelihood that he will behave in the same manner the next time you ride. That doesn't mean you should expect a horse to behave flawlessly every time he's ridden. But, even when he is having a bad day, try to find something that he does well to end on.

There are, of course, numerous additional ways to reward horses as discussed in Chapter II. A gentle stroke with the hand, a softly spoken word and an opportunity to graze are all things that can reinforce bad behavior, just as they can increase responsiveness to aids. The only difference is when the reward is given, make sure that it follows desirable, not undesirable, behavior.

Why Do It if There Isn't a Payoff?

Since horses behave in undesirable ways to acquire rewards, it follows that an undesirable behavior will abate—or what learning theorists call "extinguish"—if it is not rewarded. If you stop getting a paycheck, you are not likely to continue to go to work. Animals are no different. They will stop doing something if there isn't a payoff. Thus, you can prevent or eliminate undesirable behaviors simply by averting the reward. The most generally useful method for accomplishing that while riding is through corrections.

GOLDEN RULE #8

Undesirable Behavior Extinguishes if It Is Not Rewarded

Correct Rather Than Punish

Often, our first inclination is to punish horses when they do something we don't like. Reward them for doing the right thing; punish them for doing the wrong thing. At first blush, it seems like a logical formula for shaping behavior. The problem is that punishment by definition implies rough handling and the infliction of physical or mental discomfort. There is nothing either gentle or tactful about it. In addition, more often than not, punishment is precipitated by a loss of self-discipline and patience, coupled with the frustration of not knowing how to deal with the problem more rationally. Even when that is not the case, punishment seldom accomplishes its intended purpose, and it can create more problems than it solves.

All the same, I am not advocating that you condone disagreeable behavior. Horses should always be immediately corrected when they do something objectionable. But, don't think that the word "correction" is merely a euphemism for punishment. As described below, the two concepts differ in very significant ways.

Corrections Should Not Be Punishing

In effect, undesirable behavior is anything a horse does under saddle other than what the rider would like him to do. It might be a mere shift in the horse's balance or body alignment or a change in direction, speed or gait. It could be something that is viewed as more severe like bucking or rearing. Regardless of its exact nature, undesirable behavior is essentially anything a horse does that is inconsistent with the rider's wishes. The intent of a correction is solely to return the horse to doing what the rider wants. I cannot overemphasize that the rider's aim should never be to cause the horse pain or even discomfort.

When making a correction, the aids should be used tactfully and at the minimal intensity required to expeditiously counteract the undesirable behavior. In contrast to when a signal is given for a new response, it is not necessary to give a subtle signal when making a correction. A rider should be able to judge fairly accurately how potent to make the correction based on the strength of the horse's resistance. However, if the initial signal is insufficient, its potency should be increased progressively until the horse responds. Get the job done as promptly as possible. Nevertheless, the more gently a correction is made, the better. If a subtle signal is sufficient, so be it. *A correction discourages undesirable behavior because it prevents the horse from attaining the reward, not because it punishes the horse.* If the reward for an undesirable behavior is consistently blocked, the horse's motivation is nullified.

For example, as mentioned above, horses often change gaits spontaneously to conserve energy. Within each gait there is an optimal range of speed that allows horses to travel a given distance while expending the least amount of energy. As a horse's speed increases or decreases from the optimal range, it becomes more energy efficient to change gaits. For instance, a moderate canter is more energy efficient than a fast trot. Therefore, as a horse accelerates at the trot, he reaches a speed at which it is easier for him to canter than to trot and, therefore, he instinctively begins to canter. The reward for the gait change is the conservation of energy; basically, it's easier for the horse.

Even though it is natural for horses to change gaits to save energy, it, obviously, is undesirable under saddle; a horse should change gaits only when the rider signals for him to do so. The correction for an unwanted gait change is to return the horse to the desired gait and speed. If the correction is made expeditiously, the horse doesn't reap the benefits of the gait change and consequently, with repetition, he will stop attempting to do it. In essence, he learns that he cannot conserve energy by changing gaits. A correction is Golden Rule #8 (Undesirable behavior extinguishes if it is not rewarded) put into practice.

The same logic applies to every undesirable behavior. If you can counteract the horse's attempt to misbehave, it prevents the misbehavior from being rewarded and, as a result, with repetition the behavior extinguishes. Here is another example: Horses are naturally inclined to grab a bite of foliage or grass while being ridden on trails. Often riders respond by scolding the horse. Instead, the correction would be to simply use the reins to prevent the horse from reaching his goal—a bite of food in this case—and return him to doing what he should be doing. Sound easy? It is, really! Just stay alert for any hint that the horse is starting to misbehave and then tactfully counteract it using the aids. Try to detect the misbehavior in its germinal stage. It is much more effective to correct horses at the instant they begin to misbehave than it is after the behavior has progressed further.

As you make a correction, stay focused on what you want the horse to do; don't dwell on what he did that was objectionable. The quality of a good correction is dependent on the rider and not the horse. The more intensely the rider focuses on getting the horse to do what is desired, the better the correction is likely to be. Dwelling on the nature of what the horse did to prompt the correction serves absolutely no functional purpose and compromises the quality of the correction by distracting the rider from the task at hand. Later, especially if the horse actually did something truly contumacious, i.e., obstinately disobedient or rebellious, it is often advisable to reflect on the circumstances under which the undesirable behavior occurred. Almost always, if you can figure out why it occurred, it will tell you how to prevent or eliminate it. However, the best time for such analysis is after you have dismounted. While riding, your attention should be wholly consumed with getting the horse to do what you want him to do. And, don't violate the golden rules described in Chapter II. Make sure that you are not the cause of the undesirable behavior.

Corrections Suppress Undesirable Behavior Permanently; Punishment Does Not

When the reward for an undesirable behavior is repeatedly foiled by corrections, the offense is likely to appear less and less frequently, and the horse's commitment to doing it will become less earnest. The horse might continue to do it now and then for some time, particularly when the circumstances that initially elicited it are more intense than usual.

For example, in the beginning of his training under saddle, Gabriel bolted when, in his opinion, he was working too hard. He'd drop his outside shoulder and run toward that direction.[13] Many times riders respond to such a maneuver by pulling on the inside rein. It is natural, for example, to pull on the left rein when a horse bolts toward the right. However, by dropping the outside shoulder and over bending at the withers, the horse essentially nullifies the power of the inside aids. Consequently, the horse can continue to run despite the rider's efforts to stop him. It is much better to use the outside aids in such situations. The action of the rider's outside leg combined with a fixed outside hand, lifts the horse's outside shoulder and straightens him. All of the aids then become effective and, therefore, the rider is able to immediately return the horse to doing what he was doing prior to bolting.

Each time Gabriel bolted, I corrected him. As his attempts to bolt were repeatedly thwarted, he tried to do it less and less often. As time went by, he rarely attempted to bolt and, frankly, even when he did try, his heart really was not in it. Then, after two years without a single attempt, he tried it one more time on an exceptionally hot and humid day when we were working on movements that required both strength and agility. Once again, I made the correction and we went back to work.

You are likely to have similar experiences. There is nothing magical about corrections. A correction often must be repeated quite a few times to eliminate an undesirable behavior entirely. Don't become frustrated even if a misbehavior reemerges anew after a period of time. If you consistently and effectively correct a horse, eventually the undesirable behavior will permanently disappear from his repertoire. Punishment, on the other hand, even at best, only suppresses undesirable behavior temporarily; it's a scientific fact.

Consider the similarity between reward and punishment. When a horse is rewarded for a particular response, it increases the likelihood that the response will be repeated. However, if the reward is withheld, then the response will extinguish over time; that principle is the basis for Golden Rule #8 (Undesirable behavior extinguishes if it is not rewarded). Said another way, responses must be rewarded periodically or they will dissipate. The same rule holds true for punishment. Like a reward, punishment must be repeated periodically to sustain its effect. In practical terms that means if you chose to deal with an undesirable behavior through punishment, then you will be destined to continue to punish the horse off and on for the offense forever.

Furthermore, there is a positive relationship between the severity of punishment and the duration of its effect. Consequently, the less severe the punishment, the more often it will have to be repeated. The same is true for rewards. That is, all other things being equal, the better the reward, the greater its impact. However, I want to make it perfectly clear that I am not advocating that it is better to severely punish a horse. I definitely and unequivocally am not. I have raised this issue only because it provides an insight into why some riders wind up "nagging" their horses. Not knowing what else to do when their horses misbehave, they punish them. However, because they are rightfully reluctant to do anything that truly causes the horse pain, the punishment is very mild. Consequently, it must be repeated over and over again making both horse and rider miserable with no positive payoff. It is far better to correct a horse which, with consistent repetition, eventually abolishes undesirable behavior permanently.

Punishment Often Has Severe Negative Side Effects, Corrections Do Not

Properly executed corrections rarely, if ever, have severe negative side effects. However, corrections do occasionally have minor consequences that riders should be aware of. The most adverse occur when horses are corrected for misbehaviors that they have been doing for some time. Then, there are three potential side effects:

One is called an "extinction burst." This refers to a sudden increase in the rate of responding after extinction begins. Essentially, when horses are accustomed to doing something, they sometimes do it even more frequently and perhaps more intensely for a short period after their attempts to do it begin to be consistently thwarted through corrections. For example, let's say that, when brought to a halt outdoors, a horse is accustomed to pulling the reins out of the rider's hands so he can eat grass. Then, the rider decides to no longer allow the horse to pull the reins away. In so doing, the horse is prevented from getting to the grass. In practice, each time the horse attempts to lower his head the bit acts as an immovable barrier. Upon meeting such a barrier, many times the horse will return his head to a normal level on his own. If he does not, the aids should be used tactfully to accomplish it. Sometimes the reins alone are sufficient to bring the horse's head back up. Other times it might require the rider to use the reins while bearing down into the stirrups for extra leverage. In any event, at first the horse's effort to get to the grass might increase rather than decrease. It's a "this always worked before" kind of reaction, and convinced from past experience that he should be able to get to the grass, the horse tries even harder. If you experience an extinction burst, don't become frustrated and lose faith in the effectiveness of corrections. Extinction bursts tend to be very short-lived. Just continue to correct the horse, and the undesirable behavior will quickly subside and eventually disappear.

Correcting a well-established misbehavior can also precipitate a strong emotional response. In essence, the horse gets frustrated upon finding that he is unable to do what he has always done before. In exceptional cases, horses can literally throw a temper tantrum under such circumstances. But again, it is an extremely rare occurrence and it only happens when the misbehavior is well ingrained. If the horse has an emotional response, do not become upset with him. Also, make absolutely sure that you do not perpetuate the emotional outburst by inadvertently rewarding it in some way. Treat it like any other undesirable behavior. That is, patiently and tactfully use the aids to return the horse to doing what you would like him to be doing. When you accomplish that, forget about the misbehavior and continue with what you were doing.

There is one more potential side effect that can be precipitated by corrections. Sometimes, when a misbehavior is corrected, horses take another approach in trying to attain their intended goal. For example, when a horse finds that his attempt to conserve energy by changing gaits is foiled, he might, instead, try to slow down to save energy. If that is foiled, he might then try to shift his balance toward his forehand to conserve energy. If that is foiled, he might then try to overbend to lighten the load on his weaker side. And so it goes. The greater a horse's motivation to attain the reward, whatever it is, the more things he is likely to try in an attempt to attain it. Again, don't become discouraged or frustrated; just keep correcting the horse. This type of inter-action between horse and rider is perfectly normal; it is the rule rather than the exception.

I envision such interchanges between horse and rider as ongoing conversations: When the horse learns that he can-not conserve energy by changing gaits, he asks whether he can do so by slowing down. The rider then answers "no" by using the aids to return the horse to the desired speed. The horse then asks whether he can shift his weight onto his fore-hand. Again, the rider says "no" by using the aids to maintain the horse in proper balance. And so the conversation between horse and rider goes. Each time, regardless of what the horse does, the rider makes the appropriate correction by returning him to doing what is desired. Through such conversations, the horse learns that each deviation from what the rider has asked wastes energy and accomplishes nothing. In the long run, he "realizes" that the most energy-efficient strategy is to simply continue to do what the rider has asked.

An adept trainer, of course, rewards such compli-ance in some way. If the horse was trying to save energy, as in the example, the perfect reward would be to give him an opportunity to rest after he did what he was asked to do for a period of time. If the horse was trying to eat on the trail, let's say, a good reward would be to allow him an opportunity to browse after a period of good performance. In essence, the horse gets what he wants most, but only on the rider's terms.

When you begin to think of rewards in this way, you might be surprised by the variety of different things that can be done to reward a horse. For example, recently while I was riding in a nearby arena, Gabriel was unusually distracted by a particular pile of manure that another horse, probably a mare, had left behind. Every time I brought Gabriel to a halt, he tried to walk over to investigate it—it's a stallion thing. Each time he tried to walk away I corrected him by backing him to where I wanted him to stand. After a number of halts with corrections, Gabriel finally stopped and stood quietly without attempting to walk over to the manure. When he did, I rewarded him by riding to the manure and allowing him to investigate it. Just keep in mind that *a reward should always be a consequence of the rider's initiative rather than that of the horse.* Don't get tricked into letting the horse do whatever he wants to do.

Punishment, in contrast to corrections, often has severe, negative side effects that do not go away. For example, sometimes punishment suppresses one undesirable behavior only to have it replaced by some type of avoidance response evoked by the horse's fear of the punishment itself. I'm sure you can think of examples. One that is notorious pertains to the misuse of the reins to punish bad behavior: It is not out of the ordinary to see a rider jerk on the reins or harshly "saw the bit" back and forth in a horse's mouth when he does something that the rider doesn't like. In the end, *horses that are punished usually adopt some chronic strategy to protect themselves.* In this case, many "go behind the bit." Others become headshy and overreactive to any movement made by the rider. Still others become "stargazers" to keep the bit positioned against the molars rather than the sensitive bars of the jaw. Horses can adopt other types of strategies to protect themselves from other types of punishment; nevertheless, it is never one that makes them more pleasant to ride.

It is also not unusual for a horse to be punished for doing one thing only to have some other desirable behavior inadvertently suppressed. Horses aren't always focused on the same thing that the rider is focused on. For example, I once watched a rider in an arena jerk on the reins every time the horse started to speed up at the trot. It didn't take long for the horse to stop trotting entirely; no matter what gesticulations the rider went through, the horse refused to trot. Apparently, the horse figured that trotting was a dangerous thing to do under the circumstances; he never made the connection between a change in tempo and the punishment.

Finally, it should be fairly obvious that punishment can have a significant negative impact on a horse's enthusiasm. I'll use an example from my own experience: Although Gabriel was already reasonably well behaved in general, he nonetheless bucked when I first began to ride him on trails. There was nothing malevolent about it; it clearly was an expression of joyfulness and exhilaration. He only did it at the very beginning of the first gallop of the day. It was as if he was saying, "Yippee! I'm free to run." Bucking of this type, that is done out of playfulness or exuberance, is sometimes referred to as capering or gamboling to distinguish it from bucking that originates from more serious causes. The truth is, when Gabriel tried to buck, it usually brought a bit of a smile to my face because I knew that I was asking him to do something that he truly enjoyed. I never punished him for it. If I did, it might have suppressed the bucking, but it also would probably have sapped some of his enthusiasm for the trail.

Put yourself in a horse's position. Would you be enthusiastic about doing something if you were punished every time you made a mistake? I can't speak for you, but I'd lose my enthusiasm for the activity pretty quickly. Horses are no different. Don't expect an enthusiastic mount if you use punishment as a training tool.

Of course, I didn't totally condone Gabriel's bucking either, so I made the appropriate correction: Horses begin to buck by markedly lowering their head and rounding their topline in an exaggerated manner. They can't buck if their head is at a normal level. Bucking can be stopped or, if you catch it early enough, prevented by bracing your weight down into the stirrups while using the reins to bring the horse's head back up to a normal level. Then, the correction is completed by immediately adjusting the horse's gait, tempo, direction, etc., as needed.

Corrections Encourage Proper Behavior; Punishment Does Not

At best, punishment only suppresses undesirable behavior. It tells the horse absolutely nothing at all about what he should do instead. Corrections, on the other hand, suppress undesirable behavior and simultaneously encourage the horse to behave properly. There are two contributing factors:

First, every correction, like any signal, should end with a release of the aids (Golden Rule #2: Signals should stop as soon as the horse begins to make an acceptable response), the primary reward for compliance with a signal. Then, the rider, of course, should harmonize with the position and movement of the horse, essentially making it as easy as possible for the horse to continue to do what he is doing and thereby minimize his motivation for doing something else.

Second, because everything else that the horse attempts to do is foiled, he learns that his best strategy is to continue to do what the rider has specified. Why continue to waste effort and energy trying unsuccessfully to do anything else? You and I don't like to waste energy and neither do horses. In this case, it motivates the horse to continue to do what the rider has asked until another signal is given.

Punishment Begins Where Knowledge Ends

There is an old saying, "Violence begins where knowledge ends." I would like to amend that saying to, "Punishment begins where knowledge ends." At its core, *punishment is really no more than ill treatment that the rider mistakenly believes will have some positive impact.* It is only logical that riders would choose another more tactful approach if they knew one. Hopefully, no rational rider actually prefers to punish a horse. Most people I know actually feel awful after punishing a horse, regardless of what the horse did to prompt it.

Nevertheless, it doesn't require any special skill or knowledge to jerk on the reins or to spur or hit a horse or even to yell at him when he does something objectionable. You don't have to have a "good seat" and you don't have to be skilled in the use of rein, leg or weight aids. To put it bluntly, it is easy to punish a horse and, for reasons that are beyond me, it seems natural for our species to lash out at

things we don't like. The futility of using punishment as a
training method is a hard lesson for us to learn, perhaps
because it goes against some basic fabric in our makeup.
Sometimes we seem to go on doing it even when it is apparent that it is counterproductive. Maybe the original offense
reemerges—remember punishment doesn't suppress behavior permanently. Even worse, maybe there is now some new
avoidance behavior to deal with brought on by the fear of
punishment. Or, maybe the horse continues to behave in the
same undesirable way, but now he also refuses to do something else that the rider would like him to do. It isn't a very
pretty picture. It is frustrating and tends to foster negative,
sometimes even hostile, feelings toward the horse.

Hopefully, I have convinced some of you to discard
punishment from your training methods. It might be helpful
to keep in mind that, more often than not, when horses do
something undesirable, they nevertheless are doing something that comes naturally to them. For example, as I have
already mentioned, changes in balance, body alignment,
speed and gait are typically nothing more than instinctual
attempts to conserve energy. Horses also instinctually scan
their surroundings for danger—shifts in attention and direction of travel are a natural consequence. Horses that try to
eat on the trail are simply following an inherent inclination
to graze at will when presented with an attractive opportunity. Some of the more rebellious and stubbornly defiant
behaviors under saddle emerge out of the natural social
urges of horses. Other "misbehavior" originates from a natural timidity and a lack of "worldly" experiences. A horse
that kicks, bites or threatens other horses when being ridden

is merely trying to protect his personal space and social status. Bucking can be an expression of exuberance and joy; when it is not, it usually is an attempt to escape pain or discomfort caused by the rider or tack. Often horses brace against riders to protect a physical weakness stemming from a conformational shortcoming and/or too little conditioning.

Still other types of misbehavior stem from the lack of training or faulty training. For instance, an insensitivity to the aids due to the lack of proper training often underlies what riders mistakenly attribute to an uncooperative nature or inherently dull senses. Sometimes undesirable behaviors are even encouraged by riders who inadvertently reward horses for doing them. Other vices, like rearing, are frequently brought on by riders who violate the golden rules for optimizing responsiveness to signals as discussed in the first section of this chapter.

Nearly 150 years ago François Baucher wrote that "...then it is the crop or whip that is used to castigate what one considers the disobedience or the hostile behavior of the horse...I uphold that the horse is never to blame...."[14] I concur completely with Master Baucher. Horses do not behave in undesirable ways because they have inherently fractious natures, and they are not inclined to work to undermine the efforts of riders. They also do not have the mental capacity to have an "agenda" as I hear said now and then when a horse behaves in an objectionable way. Scientists call such indictments anthropomorphic, that is, ascribing human motivations to the actions of horses. It is far better for a rider's mental attitude to put the "blame" where it belongs by thinking objectively about the causes of undesirable behavior, while channeling obedience and performance toward the highest levels through tactful corrections.

I would not say that all undesirable behaviors can be eliminated through corrections. After all, sometimes horses behave badly due to physical distress caused by pain, injury or a conformational shortcoming. No amount of correction will cure such problems. These are cases where the problem dissipates only when their cause is eradicated. Sometimes truly insubordinate behavior is difficult to eliminate by any means from the saddle; it stems from the natural social inclinations of horses and can only be resolved from the ground (See Chapter IV). However, perhaps in all other cases, the solution is to patiently correct, correct and correct again through the tactful use of the aids.

I like to tell riders to ride every step. By that, I mean that they should be constantly monitoring every aspect of the horse's performance and comparing it to their image of what is correct. Check his balance, body alignment, longitudinal flexion, speed, direction, point of attention, length of stride, gait, etc., and promptly set them right if they stray from where you would like them to be. *A truly good rider is not one who becomes frozen into some idealized position atop the horse; it is one who remains in harmony with the movement and position of the horse while continuously monitoring and adjusting his performance through the subtle and tactful use of the aids.*

Some riders tell me that is too much work; they would rather just relax and enjoy the ride. In response, I compare such active riding to learning to walk. Toddlers have to really work at walking; it takes a lot of conscious effort for them to stay on their feet and negotiate from here to there. But, with practice, walking soon becomes second nature, and all of the proper adjustments are made without conscious thought. Riding is very much the same. If you want to channel a horse's performance toward the highest levels, then it is your responsibility to be alert for the slightest deviations from the ideal and to counteract them. At first, it takes a lot of conscious effort but, after awhile, it becomes second nature. In the end, who do you think enjoys riding more—the person who sits and "relaxes" on his or her untrained, probably ill-mannered horse or the person who has truly trained his or her horse through tactful corrections to be easy and pleasant to ride?

Correct Without Exception

In practice, corrections are easy to do if you are skilled and knowledgeable in the use of the aids. Then, remember that corrections must be executed expeditiously to effectively thwart the horse's reward for the undesirable behavior. Beyond that, there is only one additional vital key to successfully using corrections: *An undesirable behavior must be corrected every single time that it occurs, with absolutely no exceptions for optimal effectiveness.* Each time a rider allows a misbehavior to go uncorrected it becomes that much harder to eliminate. There is a sound scientific reason for this:

Specifically, the resistance of a behavior to extinction is strongly affected by the reward schedule. *The hardest behaviors to extinguish are those that have been rewarded intermittently*—that is, now and then. Do you remember in Chapter II my assertion that the most effective strategy is to give positive rewards intermittently? It prevents the need that the reward satisfies from becoming satiated. Intermittent rewards also produce the strongest bond between the signal and the response, making the response very stable and resistant to extinction. The same thing is true for undesirable behavior. That is, if an undesirable behavior is rewarded intermittently, it becomes very resistant to extinction.

An example using people might give you an intuitive feeling of why this is so. Let's say there are two equestrians who would like to be freelance writers for horse magazines. Having an article accepted for publication, obviously, is rewarding for an aspiring author. The results for the first 12 articles that each submitted for publication are shown below:

ARTICLE #	AUTHOR A	AUTHOR B
1	*Accepted*	*Accepted*
2	*Accepted*	Rejected
3	*Accepted*	Rejected
4	*Accepted*	Rejected
5	Rejected	*Accepted*
6	Rejected	Rejected
7	Rejected	*Accepted*
8	Rejected	Rejected
9	Rejected	Rejected
10	Rejected	Rejected
11	Rejected	Rejected
12	Rejected	*Accepted*

Notice that each writer had the same number of articles accepted for publication; that is, they both were rewarded the same number of times. However, Writer A had the first four articles accepted and then the next eight in a row were rejected. Writer B, on the other hand, had the four articles accepted intermittently among the rejected articles. Do you think this difference would have an impact on the authors' psyche? Sure! Writer A is likely to be getting a little discouraged. She is probably thinking that her writing career isn't going very well and maybe that the accepted articles were beginner's luck; possibly it's time to start thinking about another career. Writer B, on the other hand, is probably thinking that some articles get published and others do not; it's just the way freelance writing is. She is likely to be feeling fairly positive after having four articles published in her burgeoning career. Perhaps more consistent success will come with more experience.

Now, if both writers had their next five articles rejected, which one do you think is most likely to give up her writing career? Writer A, right? After having 13 articles rejected in a row, she is likely to be thinking that she will never get another article published. Writer B, on the other hand, probably would just regard the stretch of rejections as one more that will pass if she continues to submit articles. After all, she has gone through stretches of rejections before.

A horse's psyche is likewise markedly influenced by the reward schedule, and he is much more likely to continue to do something if it is reinforced intermittently. That means, if, for one reason or another, you allow an undesirable behavior to go uncorrected now and then, you are, in fact, guaranteeing that the horse will continue to do it. Instead, be consistent. If you don't want a horse to do something, correct him every single time he tries to do it, regardless of the circumstances. Don't make exceptions to be "nice" to the horse or for any other reason. In the long run, it is an injustice that only confuses horses about what they can and cannot do. Keep the rules as simple as possible.

CHAPTER

IV

IMPROVING
TEMPERAMENT

Horses attain social order within a herd by forming a dominance hierarchy. The way any two individuals interact is determined largely by their rank relative to one another. Higher-ranking horses are privileged. They always have first dibs on food, water, space, etc., over subordinates. In essence, they go where they want to go and do what they want to do.

When interacting with humans, horses weigh their relative rank just as they do with other horses, and they instinctively behave accordingly. If they perceive a handler as a subordinate, they are likely to be unruly and insolent. Put yourself in their position. Are you inclined to do what your subordinates tell you to do? Not necessarily, I bet. In fact, you probably would consider it offensive if a subordinate tried to order you around. Horses are no different. They don't like to be told what to do by a lower-ranking individual either.

On the other hand, even if a horse has not been sufficiently schooled to be considered truly obedient, he is likely to be civil and compliant if he believes that you outrank him. Again, this isn't difficult to fathom. Humans, likewise, are strongly inclined to be polite and cooperative with individuals who they perceive as higher ranking, even when the individual has no true authority over them.

Before all else, then, it is crucial that a horse views you as his social superior. Otherwise, you are likely to have a contentious relationship with him. As you try to manage what he does and where he goes, he will try to assert his dominance through resistance and impertinence. He might even act aggressively toward you. It's a picture of incompatibility, with two wills at odds competing for control.

Some readers might be thinking that they would rather not dominate their horse. It's not the kind of relationship they envision. They would rather form a partnership based on mutual respect. Domination sounds so oppressive. Nonetheless, humans really do not have an option in this matter. Horses instinctively interact with other individuals according to how they perceive their relative status. It is part of their inherent makeup. They treat other individuals with respect only if they perceive them as higher ranking. Otherwise, they dismiss them with impudency. It's inevitable.

Establishing Dominance Tactfully

Horses in a herd normally establish who is dominant and who is submissive through what scientists call "agonistic encounters." In laymen's terms, they fight. However, the fighting usually doesn't cause serious injury, even to the loser. As horses have evolved, so has their behavior. Over the ages, the aggression between horses of the same herd has become ritualized to a large extent. Although some biting and kicking can occur, most agonistic encounters are limited principally to intimidation. The horse that stands his ground in the face of his opponent's aggressive posturing becomes dominant. The horse that retreats when attacked or threatened becomes subordinate.

I am not suggesting that you go out and threaten to kick and bite your horse until he retreats from you. You don't have to go that far. The key to tactfully attaining superiority over a horse lies not in how rank is initially established between horses, but in how it is manifested thereafter.

If you watch horses in a herd with an established dominance hierarchy, you will see few agonistic encounters between individuals. Once each individual recognizes his or her rank relative to each of the other members of the herd, the social environment remains rather tranquil. There is little or no friction between dominant and subordinate horses and they often stand side-by-side, play together and even physically comfort one another. However, a dominant horse always has proprietary rights to all resources, including food, water and space, over a subordinate. Subordinate horses honor those rights by freely relinquishing resources when asked. Operationally, this simply means that a subordinate always moves out of the way when asked by a higher-ranking individual. They don't have to avoid higher-ranking individuals at all costs; they just have to withdraw when the dominant horse signals them to do so. Consequently, if you can persuade a horse to withdraw at your request, that is, on cue, in his mind he will be acting submissively to you and he will naturally begin to perceive you as a higher-ranking individual.

Intention Movements

The signal given by a dominant horse to tell a subordinate to withdraw is a special type of body language called an "intention movement." Typically, there are two messages implicit to intention movements. One message is a request for the other individual to do something. The second message reveals what the individual making the intention movement is about to do. Intention movements are always actions that are preparatory to the subsequent activity or are the initial stage of the activity itself.

Horses are by no means the only species that use intention movements as signals; we do too. For example, have you ever had someone continue to talk to you when you wanted to go someplace else? If so, you might have turned your body slightly away from that person and toward the way out, or maybe you reached out and took hold of the doorknob. These are intention movements. They are preparatory for the act of actually departing. They signal the other person to bring the conversation to an end (first message) because you are about to leave (second message).

One intention movement used by horses to tell subordinates to withdraw is derived from the act of biting another horse. Essentially, it is a subtle preparatory action. Basically, the dominant horse lays his ears back a little while extending his muzzle slightly toward the subordinate horse. If the lower ranking horse doesn't move away, the dominant horse makes the signal more menacing. However, the intention movement does more than merely signal the subordinate to move away. It also carries the message "or else I will attack you," and if the subordinate does not make an acceptable response, that is exactly what will eventually happen. The higher-ranking horse will charge with ears flattened back and teeth bared. If he must actually bite the subordinate to make him withdraw, so be it.

Horses Adhere to the Golden Rules

Does anything about the dominant horse's signaling strategy strike a familiar chord? I hope so. If you look closely, you will see that *dominant horses adhere to the golden rules for optimizing sensitivity to signals when bidding a subordinate*

Shahladdinn telling Rupert to move away with an intention movement.
PHOTOGRAPHED BY THE AUTHOR.

to withdraw. Thus, they give a distinct signal (Golden Rule #4: Signals should be distinct) that tells the subordinate to move out of the way (Golden Rule #1: Aids and cues are signals for change). The signal is initially subtle, but its potency is increased if the subordinate does not make an acceptable response (Golden Rule #3: Signals should never be ignored). When the subordinate moves away, the higher ranking horse stops signaling (Golden Rule #2: Signals should stop as soon as the horse begins to make an acceptable response) and serenity is immediately restored (Golden Rule #6: Rewards enhance sensitivity to signals only when they immediately follow an acceptable response). The laws of learning are not species specific. Horses follow the golden rules elaborated in Chapter II for optimizing the sensitivity of a subordinate to their signal to withdraw, and so should you when teaching a horse to move away on cue. *It isn't enough to simply make a horse withdraw from you; dominance is established only when it can be prompted consistently by a subtle cue.*

Asking a Horse to Withdraw

If you are dealing with a horse that is truly impertinent to the point of being dangerously aggressive when handled or if you expect that he might be if pushed to do something that he would rather not do, consider having a professional take him through the initial phase of ground training. Dominance is usually transferable. That is, once a trainer establishes his or her dominance, the horse is likely to be more polite to you as well. Apparently, at least in this case, horses do not distinguish one person from another readily, although they certainly can learn to make the discrimination. In any event, if you solicit the help of a trainer, then your responsibility would be to solidify and maintain your dominance over the horse as further elaborated in the next sections. If, on the other hand, you choose to do the initial training yourself, I strongly recommend the use of a round pen. A round pen is not necessary for teaching a horse to move on cue but it allows you to work with the horse at a distance until he begins to see you as his superior. This is a definite advantage if you are training a horse that is genuinely audacious. Nevertheless, you can accomplish just as much by working with the horse at the end of some type of lunge line. I prefer to use a 12–14 foot long ⅝-inch diameter soft rope. You can make one by tying a clasp onto the end of a soft rope. I find it less awkward to handle and more effective for establishing dominance than commercially available lunge lines that are usually flat and 25–30 feet long.

Whether you are working with the horse in a round pen or on a lunge line, your body language and position relative to the horse should be your primary means for controlling the horse's movement. *Being able to control the movement of a horse from the ground goes hand-in-hand with an ability to use your body to communicate with him.* **Do not resort to verbal commands such as "walk," "trot," "canter" and "halt."** This is not a traditional lungeing exercise. Dominance can only be established through body language. There is more to it than simply controlling a horse's movement. If that was all there was to it, dominance could be established through riding. But, it cannot be. I'm sure you have seen plenty of horses that were highly trained under saddle yet disrespectful when handled from the ground.

In the beginning, your body language must be assertive and vigorous. For the training to be optimally effective, **the horse must react briskly when you signal him to withdraw.** I would even go so far as to say that it doesn't hurt to alarm him a bit. In the very beginning, he should be a little awed by your persona. An "Ooooh, all right," lazy response isn't good enough. The departure must be lively and energetic—snappy.

If you are working with the horse on a line and you get a proper response when you ask him to withdraw, be aware that, initially, it might require a fair amount of restraint to keep him from pulling away from you. You might even find it necessary to brace yourself by assuming a "tug-of-war" position. However, this should only occur in the

Gabriel and Rupert demonstrating a brisk withdrawal in a round pen (A, below) and on a line (B, facing page). Notice the strong push from the back legs. PHOTOGRAPHED BY JEAN PUTZ.

A

beginning. If you follow the golden rules, the horse will quickly learn to withdraw and circle around you without putting pressure on the rope.

Nevertheless, I cannot over emphasize that the horse should continue to depart briskly throughout the training. This is not a case where he should feel that he has a choice in the matter. If a horse chooses to leave another individual, it has little bearing on social status; if anything, it indicates a lack of regard for the other individual and, therefore, could even be an expression of dominance rather than submission.

At first, body language alone is usually not sufficient to get a brisk response from a horse, especially if he views you as a subordinate. Typically, some type of artificial aid is required. What you chose to use is up to you; it's more a matter of personal preference and convenience than anything else. Professional trainers like John Lyons and Monty

B

Roberts prefer to uncoil a rope toward horses to drive them away when working in a round pen. Pat Parelli, when working with a horse on a line, twirls the end of the rope while walking toward the horse. But, if you prefer to use a whip rather than a rope, that's fine, too. I've even seen people make horses move away by tossing arena footing toward them. The tool isn't important but the result is. The horse must move away—pronto—when asked.

Regardless of how you drive the horse away, the first phase of your motion will begin to be recognized by the horse as an intention movement as the training progresses. Let's say that you are working in a round pen and you uncoil a rope toward the horse to make him move. After you drive the horse away several times using that method, he will begin to react as soon as you raise the coiled rope toward him—he will interpret the act as an intention movement. Other types of signals will likewise evolve toward intention movements. For example, I mentioned above that I have seen people move horses away by picking up arena footing and throwing it toward the horse. In that case, the act of bending down, as in picking up footing, can become an intention movement that signals the horse to withdraw. *Signals that rely on body movements naturally evolve toward intention movements.* It doesn't matter whether you uncoil or twirl a rope, throw dirt or snap a whip to make the horse move, as the training goes on he will begin to react to the initial phase of the movement or to a movement that is preparatory to the action.

When he does, encourage it by following the golden rules elaborated in Chapter II. It is a major step toward refining communication with the horse and in establishing dominance over him. In particular, when he reacts to the intention movement, don't follow through with the full action. In fact, after you make the horse withdraw a few times, you can begin to make the intention movement by itself. Give the horse an opportunity to respond to it. If he doesn't react promptly, increase the potency of the signal by exaggerating the intention movement or by actually following through and driving the horse away. When the horse makes an acceptable response, stop signaling immediately.

That does not mean that you should take your attention away from the horse; it means that you should maintain

The "Drive Line" is an imaginary line that extends outward from the horse's girth area toward the middle of the circle. To support and encourage forward movement, a handler must stay behind that line as he or she moves on a small circle.

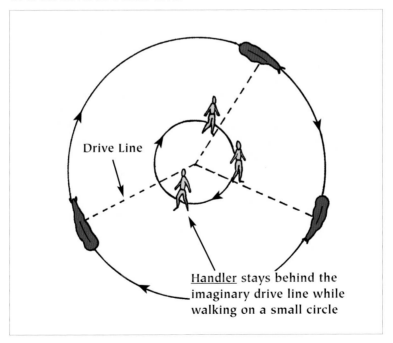

Drive Line

Handler stays behind the imaginary drive line while walking on a small circle

a body position and focus relative to the horse that supports his movement. In practice, that means that as the horse circles around you, follow his movement by walking in a small circle. As you walk, your focus and energy should be directed toward a point that is behind the horse's "drive line." The drive line is an imaginary line that extends outward from approximately the horse's girth area toward the middle of the circle. If you maintain a position behind that line as a horse circles around you, it tends to support his forward movement. If you pass in front of the drive line, it tends to make the horse turn and go in the opposite direction.

However, keep in mind that it is the horse's responsibility to continue to do what you have asked him to do until you signal for a change. In this case, that means that he should continue to circle around you, whether in a round pen or on a lunge line of some sort, until you signal for him to do something else. If the horse attempts to slow down, stop or change directions on his own, expeditiously reestablish the conditions that you originally specified. Such corrections help to impress upon the horse that you control where and how he goes and, therefore, contribute to establishing you as a higher ranking individual. With practice you will find that a horse's speed, gait and direction can all be easily dictated using body language and position relative to the horse. If you find it difficult to do at first, don't hesitate to experiment to see how changes in your body position and language affect the horse's movement.

When you ask the horse to move away from you, one or two circles around you are sufficient. Training takes place when you signal and the horse responds—remember, training is synonymous with transitions. Horses do not learn anything worthwhile by going in circle after circle with no change. A horse's sensitivity to a signal to withdraw increases only with repeated exposure to it.

In a Round Pen

The logistics of how to easily and repeatedly ask a horse to withdraw from you differs depending on whether you are training the horse in a round pen or on a lunge line. If you are working in a round pen, the most expedient way to ask for a withdrawal is to tell the horse to change directions while he is circling you. A turn is nothing more than a withdrawal toward a new direction.

To tell the horse to change directions, adjust your position relative to his so that it no longer supports his movement in the same direction but, instead, interferes with it. In practice, this means moving from a position that is behind the horse's drive line toward one that is in front of it. Change positions as if to intercept the horse's path of travel. Then, as the horse approaches, tell him to reverse directions by signaling toward his front end or slightly in front of him. For example, if you are uncoiling a rope to tell the horse to withdraw, aim a little ahead of him. Again, as the training progresses, an intention movement should become sufficient to redirect the horse's path. Ultimately, the horse should even begin to respond to a slight change in your position relative to his. Merely stepping across the drive line should be enough to cause a change in direction. Be alert for such improvements in sensitivity as the training progresses and encourage them by following the golden rules. *Always strive to use the least amount of energy necessary to get the response you want.* However, if at any time, the horse continues on in the same direction despite your signal, just wait for him to complete another revolution around you and try again with a more emphatic signal.

On a Line

If the horse is on some type of lunge line, it is easier to make him stop before signaling for a change of direction. To do so, step toward the horse with one foot as you run a hand up the line toward him. Then apply pressure on the rope by pulling back toward your bellybutton with the hand that you advanced. This causes the horse's front end to slow relative to his hind end. As a result, his hindquarters should swing outward as he comes to a stop facing toward you. If the horse is circling left, step toward the horse with your left foot and run your left hand up the line. If he is circling right, advance your right foot and hand. At first it might require strong resistance to stop the horse. However, if you follow the golden rules, eventually the horse will stop as you begin to advance your hand up the line; it becomes an intention movement.

Illustration on facing page: *When working in a round pen, ask a horse to move away from you by positioning yourself so that you can signal the horse to turn and circle in the opposite direction. This requires moving from a position behind the drive line to one that is ahead of it. Figure A illustrates that early in the training, it is usually necessary to markedly change your position relative to the horse. Move as if to intercept the horse's path of travel. As the training progresses (Figure B), merely taking a step toward the horse and ahead of the drive line should be sufficient to cause the horse to change directions.*

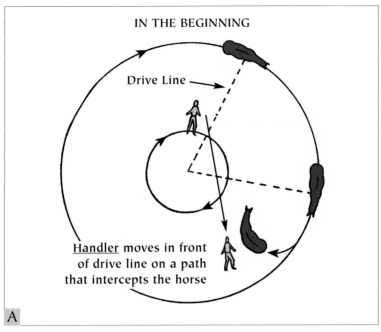

IN THE BEGINNING

Drive Line

Handler moves in front
of drive line on a path
that intercepts the horse

A

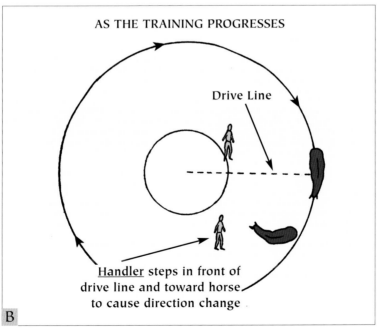

AS THE TRAINING PROGRESSES

Drive Line

Handler steps in front of
drive line and toward horse
to cause direction change

B

If the horse stops but does not turn to face you, signal him to move his haunches away **while holding his forehand in place with the line.** To move the hindquarters, signal for a withdrawal but, in this case, directed toward the point of his hip. Make the signal just vigorous enough to move the horse's hindquarters. As soon as his hindquarters begin to rotate outward, stop signaling. Then, when he is standing still and facing you, give him a second or so before asking him to move away again.

Sometimes people have difficulty making horses withdraw on a lunge line. They believe that the signal must come from the rear of the horse. Then, when they try to get into position behind the horse, he swings his hindquarters away from them by turning around his forehand. And so it goes with the handler running around the horse trying to catch up to the hindquarters.

Instead, if the horse is facing toward you, direct your signal toward the side of his neck. It might surprise you but, when a horse is facing toward you, a cue directed in front of his withers will make him move forward. Some horses briefly back away initially, but, if you do not allow it by keeping pressure on

Photos on facing page: *Stopping a horse on a line: As Rupert circled to my left I stepped toward his head with my left leg and ran my left hand up the line (A). I then applied pressure on the rope by shifting my weight backward and pulling my left hand back toward my bellybutton (B & C). This slowed Rupert's front end relative to his back end and, consequently, his hindquarters swung outward (B & C) so that he stopped and faced me (D). Notice that I allowed Rupert's movement to lessen tension on the line as he came to a halt. By making the correct response, Rupert rewarded himself by releasing pressure. With repetition, horses interpret the initial phase of the handler's action—stepping forward and running a hand up the line—as an intention movement, and they halt even before pressure is applied.* PHOTOGRAPHED BY JEAN PUTZ.

the line while you continue to signal, the horse will quickly modify his strategy and go forward to your left or right. If you want the horse to move off toward your left, signal toward the left side of his neck. If you want him to move off toward your right, signal toward the right side of his neck. In either case, be aware that the horse's forward movement might be explosive the first time or so that you use this technique. **Do not stand directly in front of him when you signal.**

Signs of Submission

As you are teaching a horse to move away, there are several signs that will tell you that the training is going well. For example, you might see the horse stick out his tongue in a sort of licking motion. I am not sure of the exact meaning of this gesture; different people ascribe different messages to it. It bears some resemblance to the mouthing movements that immature horses sometimes make as they approach or are approached by an adult. Whether the two gestures are related remains to be determined. In any event, both appear to be signs of submissiveness.

You might also see the horse go from a high-headed, hollow-backed carriage to a more rounded one with his head lower. Eventually, he may even stretch his neck downward so his muzzle is only a few inches above the ground. All animal

Photos on facing page: *Signaling for a withdrawal on a line: A horse that is standing facing toward you on a line will move off toward your left and circle left if you signal toward the left side of his neck. Hold the line in your left hand and signal with your right (A). He will move off toward your right and circle right if you signal toward the right side of his neck. In this case, hold the line in your right hand and signal with your left hand (B). Do not stand directly in front of the horse when you signal.* PHOTOGRAPHED BY JEAN PUTZ.

A

B

species that form dominance hierarchies have ritualized postures that signal others that they surrender. Scientists call them submissive postures. Fighting between male mice, for example, ends when one mouse sits up rigidly on his haunches with one foreleg stiffly extended and the other drawn back. It is a signal that says to the other mouse, "I yield to your authority."[15] The muzzle-to-the-ground posture shown by horses bears some characteristics of a submissive posture, and the context in which it normally occurs suggests that it might be one. However, submissive postures are normally muscularly rigid, and that is not the case for the muzzle-to-the-ground posture. Also, submissive postures usually involve some degree of turning away from the dominant animal, which is generally regarded as a ritualization of the intention movement to flee. Horses that assume the muzzle-to-the-ground posture do not normally turn away and may even turn toward the other individual. Moreover, often submissive postures expose a vulnerable area of the body to the dominant individual. Again, that is not the case with the muzzle-to-the-ground posture, although one could argue that it bears a marked resemblance to the posture horses assume when preparing to lay down and, therefore, it could be a ritualized intention movement for assuming that vulnerable position.

In any event, the most unambiguous sign of a horse's submission to you is his sensitivity to your signal to withdraw. When he begins to react to your intention movements,

---

Illustrations on facing page: *When a horse is standing facing toward you on a line, ask him to go forward by signaling toward the side of his neck. Do not stand directly in front of him. If you signal toward the left side of the horse's neck, he will go forward to your left and circle left (A). If you signal toward the right side of his neck, he will go forward to your right and circle right (B).*

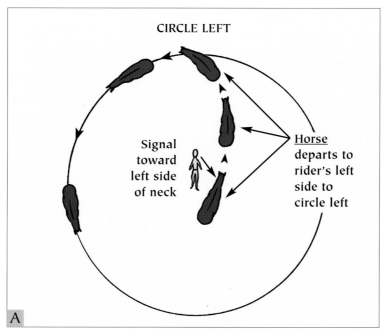

CIRCLE LEFT

Signal toward left side of neck

Horse departs to rider's left side to circle left

A

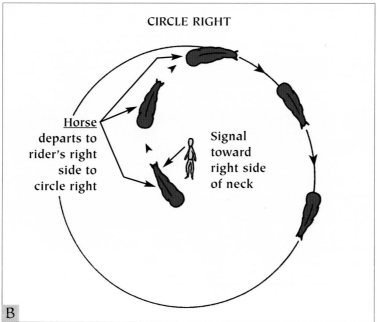

CIRCLE RIGHT

Horse departs to rider's right side to circle right

Signal toward right side of neck

B

you can be certain that you have taken a major step toward convincing the horse that you outrank him. With experience, you can reach this point rather quickly and in a single training session. However, keep in mind that there is always another day. Never exhaust the horse and jeopardize his health. There is no law that says that you must teach a horse to withdraw on cue in a single session.

Solidifying Dominance

Attention and Social Status

If you watch a herd of horses with an established dominance hierarchy, one of the things you might notice is that horses pay close attention to individuals that outrank them. If they don't, they run the risk of missing a subtle signal to withdraw and, consequently, of being attacked, literally, without warning. You, likewise, probably pay close attention to people who you perceive to have a higher rank. Have you ever attended a

Gabriel fixed his inside ear on Lynn as she worked with him on a line. This is one of the earliest signs that the horse is paying closer attention to the handler. PHOTOGRAPHED BY THE AUTHOR.

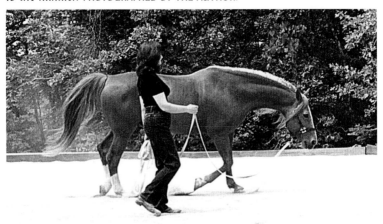

dinner party with a group of people from the office? If you have, I bet you watched and listened more closely to your boss than to your peers. It's normal to pay special attention to those who have the potential to affect your welfare.

Typically, at the beginning of training in a round pen, horses assume a high-headed, hollowed back position and orient toward the outside as they circle around the handler (A). As the training progresses, their topline becomes more rounded and their orientation shifts from the outside to the inside of the round pen as they pay closer attention to the handler (B). PHOTOGRAPHED BY JEAN PUTZ.

As you establish dominance over a horse, he will naturally pay closer attention to you. This should be evident from the horse's demeanor, but there are a few specific signs that you can look for. In particular, as the horse circles around you, he is likely to stop scanning the surroundings with his inside ear (the ear on the inside of the circle) and fix it toward you. He might also bend his neck slightly so that he is facing more toward the inside, rather than the outside, of the circle to get a better view of you. Also, when stopped, he should be more attentive to your every move. If you are working in a round pen, he might keep an eye on you as you move around the pen or he might even actually follow you. If the horse is on a lunge line, you might find that you can no longer walk to his side or behind him because he turns to keep track of you. However, the most unequivocal sign that a horse is paying attention to you is his consistent responsiveness to subtle cues. There is no way that he can respond to a subtle cue to move away if his attention is elsewhere.

Photos on facing page: *Typically, at the beginning of training on line, horses assume a high-headed, hollowed back position and they orient toward the outside as they circle around the handler (A). As the training progresses, their topline becomes more rounded and their orientation shifts from the outside to the inside of the circle as they begin to pay closer attention to the handler (B & C). A well-trained horse that views a handler as a leader becomes so focused on the handler that he is drawn inward (C). This is a huge step toward being able to train the horse completely without restraining devices. The trainer literally becomes a magnet that draws the horse to him or her. Some observant readers might have noticed that Gabriel's ears are somewhat back in the third photograph. This is frequently misinterpreted and can lead to the mishandling of a horse. It's a sign of submission, not aggression. Only when the ears are laid back with the muzzle extended forward is it a sign of aggression—then it's an intention movement that signals for withdrawal.* PHOTOGRAPHED BY JEAN PUTZ.

A

B

C

You can further solidify your dominance by teaching the horse to pay even greater attention to you. Remember that dinner party that I mentioned above? If your boss's boss was also at the table, I bet you would be even more attentive to him or her than to your boss. Social rank and level of attention are positively correlated. The greater an individual's rank, the more attention he or she commands. The converse is also true, at least in a horse's mind. That is, as you gain more of his attention, he will see your rank and authority over him as progressively more indisputable.

Teaching a Horse to be Attentive

There is nothing mystical about teaching a horse to pay close attention to you. Once again, it is merely a matter of following the golden rules for optimizing responsiveness to signals. In this case, you give a signal and the horse responds by directing his attention toward you, that is, by looking at you, preferably with both eyes.

Some sort of sound makes an ideal signal for telling a horse to pay attention. Horses can hear a sound even when they are facing away and paying attention to something else. The sound you use is arbitrary. It could be a kissing, clicking or clucking sound, but if you want to slap the side of your leg, clap your hands or whistle, be my guest. I know one trainer who stamps his feet as in flamenco dancing to get the attention of horses he trains. The nature of the sound is rather insignificant.

Regardless of what sound you choose, you can facilitate the training by pairing it with your cue for withdrawal. That is, as you teach the horse to withdraw on cue as described in the sections above, make the sound simultaneously with the signal to move away. Keep making the sound until the horse actually withdraws. Don't make the sound incessantly, only as you are signaling for him to withdraw. For example, if you uncoil a rope toward the horse to make him move away, make the sound as you do so or as you make the intention movement for driving him away. As the training progresses, the sound will naturally evolve into a cue for attentiveness. You can begin to train the signal more specifically when you see clear signs that the horse recognizes you as a higher ranking individual— in particular, when he is consistently responding to subtle cues to move away.

Then, follow the golden rules laid out in Chapter II for optimizing sensitivity to cues. At first, work with the horse standing still. Then if he is paying attention to something other than you, give the signal (Golden Rule #1: Aids and cues are signals for change). If the horse doesn't respond by redirecting his attention toward you, make the signal more emphatic (Golden Rule #3: Signals should never be ignored). To do that, repeat the sound accompanied by the cue, i.e., intention movement for withdrawal. If the horse still doesn't look at you, increase the potency even further by making the sound and following through with the intention movement to make the horse withdraw. If at any point while you are signaling the horse redirects his attention toward you, stop signaling immediately and stand quietly (Golden Rule #2: Signals should stop as soon as the horse begins to make an acceptable response).

If it is actually necessary to make the horse withdraw, after one or two circles ask him to stop. If you are working with him on a lunge line, by this point, you should have a specific cue to signal for a halt (see discussion in previous section). You are not likely to have a specific cue for stopping the horse if you are working in a round pen. In that case, the first thing to try is to simply allow the horse to stop by shifting your body language and position to neutral so that it no longer supports his forward movement. After the training has progressed this far, horses often stop fairly quickly if you simply stand quietly and relaxed in the center of the round pen. If he doesn't stop within a reasonable period of time, say within a trip or so around you, move toward a position that intercepts his path of travel as you did when telling him to withdraw in a new direction. Then, as he approaches you, give the intention movement to withdraw but less vigorously than required to actually make the horse turn; give it just strong enough to bring him to a halt. You can adjust the potency of the intention movement by changing its magnitude and quickness—the smaller and slower the movement, the less potent the signal. You can also reduce the potency of the signal by averting your eyes away from those of the horse and by turning your body so that it is not squarely toward the horse. Also try taking a step or two backward away from the horse at the instant he begins to slow down to make the turn. With some experimentation, you will find it easy to manipulate the potency of the signal so it brings the horse to a halt.

If the horse stops and stands looking at you with both eyes, just stand quietly—reward him for paying attention to you by allowing him to rest and relax. However, if he is looking anywhere other than toward you after he stops, signal for his attention.

Paying Attention Should Be Easy for the Horse

In the beginning, the easiest way for a horse to pay attention to you is if you are standing directly in front of him (Golden Rule #5: A response should be easy for the horse to make). Position yourself accordingly so he can look at you without bending his neck. If the wall of the round pen prevents you from getting directly in front of him, get as close to that position as possible, but always give yourself plenty of space so you are not in danger if the horse does something unexpected.

Even if you are standing directly in front of the horse, don't expect his attention to be riveted on you at first. You can be sure that as time passes his focus will shift to other things in the vicinity. When it does, signal to regain it by making the sound you have chosen as your cue for attention. If he does not redirect his attention toward you, make the signal more emphatic as described above. Each time you lose his focus, do the same; do it as often as necessary. With repetition the horse's attention span will become longer, and the cue needed to get his attention back when it drifts will become progressively more subtle if you follow the golden rules.

Becoming the Leader

Why the Horse's Front Feet Must Move

When you feel that you have a reasonable command of the horse's attention, you can move on to the next phase of training. If you have been working with the horse on a line, remove it. But make sure the horse can't just run away from you. He should be in some kind of enclosed area, like a round pen or an arena. A small paddock would also be fine.

Then change your position relative to the horse. Move from standing in front of him to a position a little to his side. Take a step or two to the right or left, as if the horse is standing in the center of a circle and you are taking a few steps one way or the other on the circumference of the circle. By doing so, you change your position relative to the front of the horse but not your distance from him. The ultimate goal is to get the horse to pay attention and follow you no matter where you go. But don't ask for too much at first. The farther and faster you move, the more difficult it is for

The drawing shows a handler changing from a position that is directly in front of the horse to one that is a step or two around the horse—as if he or she moved on the circumference on an imaginary circle around the horse. By doing so, the handler's distance from the horse remains about the same. The horse should continue to focus his attention on the handler as he or she moves to the new position.

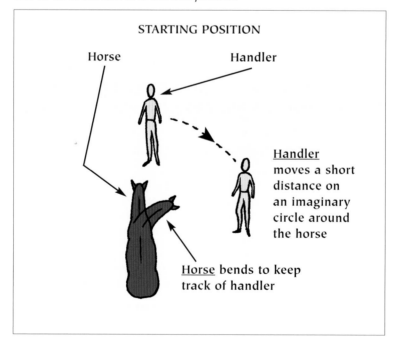

STARTING POSITION

Horse　　　　　　Handler

Handler moves a short distance on an imaginary circle around the horse

Horse bends to keep track of handler

the horse to track you. If you lose his attention at any point during the training, signal to get it back. When you do, keep in mind that the closer you are to the horse's side, the harder it is for him to look at you. Thus, especially early on, it helps to move a little more toward the front of the horse as you signal to regain his attention (Golden Rule #5: A response should be easy for the horse to make).

If the horse actually moves his feet to keep track of you as you change positions, that's great; you're ahead of the game. It is more likely, though, that initially his feet will stay stationary while he bends his neck to look at you. If that's the case, stay in your new position for a while. If you stand for a period of time watching something toward your side, eventually you will turn to face it; it is easier than standing with your neck bent, and it gives you a better view of what you are looking at. Horses do likewise. In time he will become uncomfortable with his neck bent, and it will be easier for him to turn his body to face you straight on.

When he does, there are three ways he can do it: He can rotate his hindquarters around his forehand, his forehand around his hindquarters or he can rotate around his center. This might seem like a trivial difference but, in practice, it is not. For reasons described in the following paragraph, it is important that the horse moves his front feet when he turns to face you. Some horses do this naturally, others do not. In some rare cases, horses stick to the strategy of rotating their hindquarters around their forehand so steadfastly that it almost seems as if their front feet are glued to the ground. If you find that to be the case, try to encourage the horse to move his front feet by varying your position relative to the horse as you signal for his attention: move slightly closer or farther away, or a little more to the right or left. Simultaneously, a very subtle signal to withdraw can also help to break the front feet loose. Don't signal so strongly that the horse actually withdraws—just strong enough to get a front foot to move. Again, with some experimentation and practice, you will find that it is not difficult to do. But remember, throughout the entire process make sure that you keep the horse's attention fixated on you. He should be looking at you continuously with both eyes. Changing your position relative to the horse or signaling him to withdraw won't do any good if he isn't paying attention to you.

If you watch horses begin to walk forward, you will see that they almost always begin by taking a step with a front foot. Once a horse moves his front feet laterally to follow your movements toward his right or left, it requires only a small modification in the direction of his step to get him to follow you as you walk away from him. It is the beginning of what I think of as bonding. It is a point of psychological transition at which the horse goes from viewing you as his superior to viewing you as his leader. Dominant individuals are not necessarily leaders. Leaders, on the other hand, always

Photos on facing page: After working with Rupert for a while, I tossed the rope over his back to make sure he was paying attention to me and not just following the lead rope (it would have been better to remove the rope entirely). I then moved a short distance to my right, around Rupert counterclockwise. Notice that he initially kept track of me by bending his neck (A). Then, after standing for a short time with his neck bent, he decided it would be easier to pay attention to me by turning to face me straight on. Notice that he started the turn by stepping with his left front foot (B). PHOTOGRAPHED BY JEAN PUTZ.

A

B

outrank their followers. As you teach a horse to withdraw on cue, you also take the first step toward establishing yourself as his leader.

The Benefits and Responsibilities of Leadership

The concepts of dominance and leadership differ in subtle, yet significant ways. I believe we all have an intuitive understanding of the difference between a boss and someone who we consider a leader. Likewise, there are distinct benefits associated with both. With dominance comes respect and compliance. With leadership comes a special psychological reliance. I do not mean that the horse becomes an unthinking slave with no will to act on his own. I mean that he will look to you for companionship and guidance, and he will be less fearful of his surroundings in your presence.

I remember a time when I was standing in a large pasture talking with a friend while our five horses grazed nearby. Then something spooked the herd and they quickly galloped off out of sight—all except my horse, Moment. She came over to stand close by me. If you know anything at all about herd behavior, I'm sure you recognize this as an extraordinary thing for a horse to do. It is even more remarkable because Moment was not renowned for her bravery and was prone to flight. Apparently she saw me as her "safe base," a place where she felt secure and out of harm's way. I was very proud of my relationship with her on that occasion, but this is just one small example of the kind of bond that emerges as a horse begins to recognize you as a leader and companion. Unfortunately, I admit that I am unable to describe all of the benefits that accompany such a social position; quite frankly, it is beyond my talent at this point to do the topic justice. Suffice it to say that *if you want a truly special relationship with a horse, you must aspire to be his leader, not just his boss or provider.*

Of course leadership doesn't come without a cost. There are responsibilities that accompany the status. A true leader always puts a follower's well-being before all else including his or her self-gratification or glorification. It goes beyond giving the horse sufficient food and water and a comfortable place to live. It also means seeing that he gets sufficient exercise to keep him physically and mentally fit and that there is sufficient variety in his environment and daily routine

At the end of a "photo session" in the round pen, Gabriel walked up to me and buried his head in my chest for a friendly hug. PHOTOGRAPHED BY JEAN PUTZ.

to keep his mind active and alert. And, never betray the horse's trust by abusing his willingness to comply with your wishes by asking him do anything that overtaxes him or that he can't do safely. Treat him respectfully and kindly while keeping his health and welfare of paramount importance.

How to Become a Horse's Leader

It is not difficult to achieve leadership once a horse tracks your lateral movements by moving his front feet. It is just a matter of getting him to follow you no matter where you go. But it is important that he follows you by his own volition. If he is following you because you are leading him with a lead rope, it does not have the same psychological impact. He must decide to follow you when, in fact, he could freely choose to do otherwise. If you can convince him to follow you of his own volition, he will begin to see you as his leader. It's that simple. If you can convince a horse that you are his social superior by acting like one, it shouldn't be surprising that you can also convince him that you are his leader by encouraging him to treat you as such.

When the training has progressed to this point, teaching the horse to follow after you entails using your body position relative to him to modify the direction that he steps with his front feet to keep track of you. He already moves his front feet laterally to keep track of you as you move around toward his right or left. For him to follow after you requires a transi-

Illustration on facing page: *The drawing shows a handler spiraling away in order to encourage the horse to follow along as he or she walks directly away from the horse. The ultimate goal is to have the horse follow along no matter where the handler goes.*

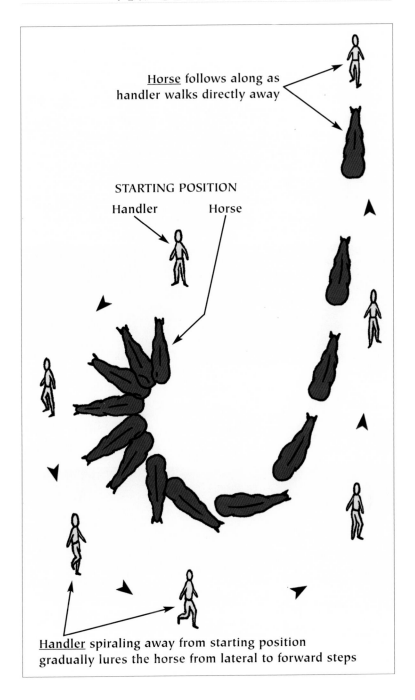

<u>Horse</u> follows along as handler walks directly away

STARTING POSITION

Handler   Horse

<u>Handler</u> spiraling away from starting position gradually lures the horse from lateral to forward steps

Photos on these two facing pages: *These photographs are a continuation of the series shown on page 109. After Rupert turned to face me by moving his front feet, he followed along as I spiraled outward to my left; notice our tracks in the sand (A). After a while, I changed directions, spiraling to my right (B). I continued to change directions (C & D) and progressively lessened the curvature of the spiral (D). Early in the training, changes of direction help to keep a horse's attention. Also, a change in direction is often all that is needed to regain a horse's attention when it begins to drift away. If it isn't, add the verbal cue for attention and, if necessary, the intention movement for withdrawal. Eventually, Rupert followed along as I walked directly away from him with a pleased grin on my face (E).* PHOTOGRAPHED BY JEAN PUTZ.

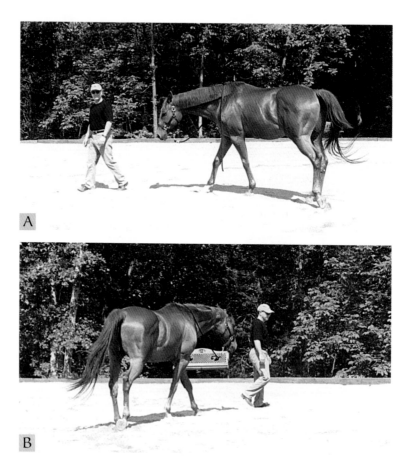

A

B

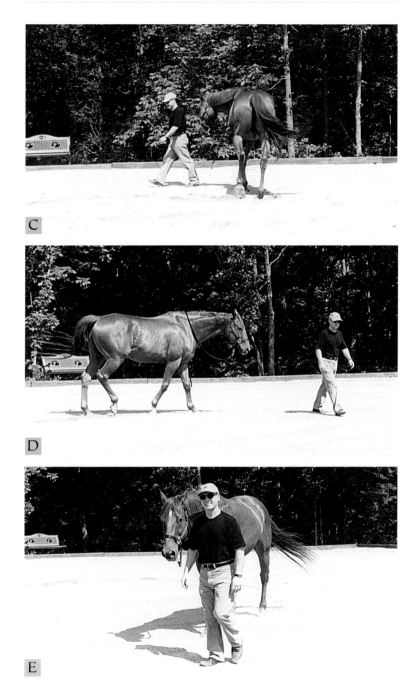

C

D

E

tion from taking lateral steps to taking forward steps. But don't start by walking straight away from the horse. To go from a lateral step directly to a forward step is a difficult transition for some horses to make. Instead, at first, try moving a little farther away from the horse as you move to the left or right around him—as if you are spiraling out from the horse's original position. Don't go too far at first. Take a few steps and stop. If the horse follows along, great! If he doesn't, take a step backward in the training and work more on getting him to follow your lateral movements around him. Then, try spiraling away again. Build slowly from moving laterally around the horse to directly walking away from him.

When you reach a point where the horse follows you regardless of the direction that you go, spend time with him doing it; the more time you spend the better. Make the training dead solid. Ingrain the idea that all is well when he pays attention to you and follows your lead. Let him discover that you are his "safe base" and that as long as he is with you he has nothing to worry about. If he stops following along at any point, immediately signal for his attention and reestablish your leadership. The more alert you are to slight deviations and the quicker you make corrections, the better. But it is important that you stay casual and relaxed. Don't make the horse edgy. You should view this time as an opportunity for the horse to learn that his environment is tranquil when he is with you.

The Versatile Attention Cue

Have you ever noticed how many different ways a dog's name can be used? I have a close companion who I'm awfully fond of. He's a 14 year old Australian Shepherd who I call Tucker.

When I ask him to do something, I sometimes say his name before the command—"Tucker, Sit." Other times, though, I just use his name by itself; like when I want him to come to dinner. Then all that I have to do is call out "Tucker" in a happy, enthusiastic voice, and shortly thereafter he shows up in the kitchen beaming with anticipation. Other times I use his name to tell him to stop what he's doing. For example, a short crisp "Tucker" always stops him dead in his tracks when he's chasing a cat. And there are also those rare occasions when I catch him "in the act"—doing something he knows he shouldn't be doing. Oh, he knows all right, I can see it in his sheepish eyes as he scans the surroundings watching for the "law" to show

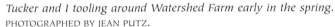

Tucker and I tooling around Watershed Farm early in the spring.
PHOTOGRAPHED BY JEAN PUTZ.

up. Like when I find him eating an "unmentionable" out in the barnyard. Then "Tucker" spoken with shoulders dropped and an air of disappointment embarrasses him enough to stop him from doing the dastardly deed again for a while.

But it's not just dog names. Our names, likewise, can carry many messages. For example, my mother has always called my father "Hon," short for Honey, I suppose. "Hon" said with just the right inflection accompanied by the appropriate expression is all that is required to communicate her approval or disapproval. A sharply spoken "Hon" brings all ongoing activity to a halt. "Hon" spoken with urgency is an alert for an impending mishap.

Can you guess why a name can be so useful? It's not just because it identifies a certain individual. It's because, when used as in the examples above, it is a signal for attention. It tells the individual to stop whatever he or she is doing and pay attention. Don't you immediately shift your attention when your name is spoken? Of course you do! So do I. I even find it difficult to ignore my name when I know it's being used to address someone else. It's a reflex-like response that's hard to suppress.

There is more to it though. The name gets the individual's attention, then the context adds a more specific message. As in the examples given above, a change in the speaker's intonation, inflection or body language, or the circumstances of the situation can vastly alter the meaning of a spoken name. It is these variables that add specificity and enrich the message making an individual's name so versatile.

It might surprise you, but as you teach a horse to pay attention to you, the voice cue you use as a signal takes on some of the characteristics of a name. It doesn't identify the horse as a particular individual. But, in conjunction with the context in which it is given and nuances added by your voice and body language, the cue for attention can take on a number of different meanings that horses readily learn to discriminate. In so doing, the cue for attention evolves into a simple, versatile means for influencing a horse's behavior from the ground and from the saddle.

For example, once a horse consistently follows you and shifts his focus to you when asked, he is also likely to come to you when you give the cue for his attention. The signal for attention naturally evolves into a signal to come to you as the horse makes the psychological transition from viewing you only as a superior to viewing you as his leader. In fact, all of the social cues tend to transform toward signals to come as you become the horse's leader. That means that if the horse doesn't come when you signal for his attention, signal again and increase its potency by adding the intention movement for the horse to withdraw. Simultaneously, take a step or so to the horse's right or left to get the front feet moving if necessary. If he still doesn't come, repeat all of the above and then follow through to drive the horse away. Run toward him if you have to, but stop in your tracks as soon as he begins to move. If the training was successful, the horse might retreat a step or so but then he will turn and come to you. It isn't magic; social cues and tendencies naturally evolve that way.

When working with the horse from the ground, the cue for attention also can be given just before a more specific signal. It alerts the horse to pay attention—as in "Tucker,

Sit." As a result he will be more sensitive to signals given subtly, like those asking him to move right, left, backward or forward. But the attention cue doesn't have to be given before every command. It isn't necessary if the horse is already paying attention to you. On the other hand, if you think a signal didn't get a response because the horse was focused on something else and just didn't notice it, rather than increasing the potency of the signal itself, get the horse's attention as you give the subtle cue again. If he still doesn't respond, increase the potency of the signal until he does. For example, I ask my horses to lift a foot by lightly

As I walked up to Gabriel, I gave a verbal cue for his attention (A). He didn't respond, so I raised my right hand toward his haunches, an intention movement for withdrawal (B). That got his attention. He promptly lifted his head (C & D), turned to face me by stepping with his left front foot (E) and walked to me (F). PHOTOGRAPHED BY JEAN PUTZ.

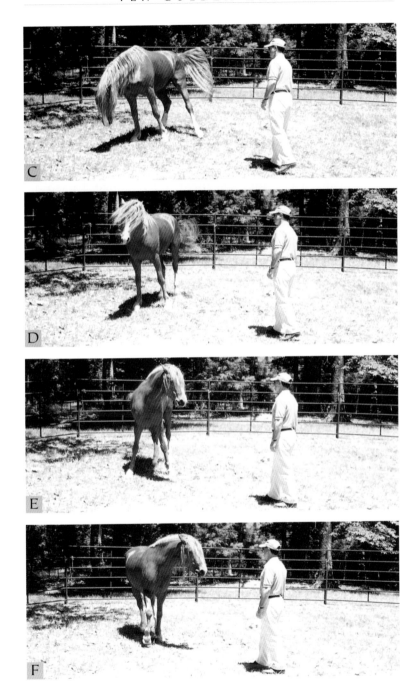

tapping on their leg. If I tap and don't get a response, I ask for their attention as I lightly tap again. If the horse still doesn't lift his foot, I tap progressively harder until he does.

The cue for attention can also be used to stop horses from doing things that you don't want them to do. Most of the time horses automatically stop what they are doing when they hear the attention cue—like when I stop Tucker from chasing a cat. Just last night, for instance, I used an attention cue to stop a small fracas between two horses on opposite sides of a fence. It's normal to stop what you are doing when your name is called out.

I also use my cue for attention to correct horses under certain circumstances. Remember, the term "correction" is not a euphemism for "punishment." A correction tactfully returns a horse to doing what he should be doing. I'll give you two examples. First, I use it to correct a horse that does something I don't want him to do while I'm leading him. Let's say he tries to stop and eat grass. As soon as does, I signal for his attention. If he responds as he should, his head will come back up so that he looks at me with both eyes. He should also be ready to resume following me of his own volition as in the training described in the preceding section and without me tugging and pulling on the lead rope. If he doesn't stop eating grass, I make the signal more emphatic by adding the intention movement or, if necessary, the full signal to withdraw. I don't stop signaling until he is paying attention to me.

Here is another example: I don't usually tie Gabriel when I groom him at home; I just walk out into his paddock with brush in hand. Early on, Gabriel would stand still for a short period while I groomed him but then he would wonder off. As soon as he began to move, I'd give his cue for attention to stop him in his tracks. If he didn't stop, I'd increase the signal potency by adding the intention movement to drive him away. If he still didn't stop, I'd increase the potency of the signal even further by increasing the magnitude of the intention movement or by following through and driving him away a few steps. Then, I'd let him stop and I'd start grooming again. If he strolled away again, I'd repeat the sequence. I did it as often as necessary until he stood quietly. With repetition, he learned that his best strategy is to stand still until I'm finished grooming him. He wasn't getting to go anywhere anyway so why keep trying?

The cue for attention can also be used when riding. Often it is all that is needed to refocus a horse that has been distracted by something in the surroundings. The cue doesn't have to be given loudly. If the horse has become sensitive to the cue during the ground work, it usually is sufficient to whisper it.

Maintaining Your Social Status

To me, the term "dominance hierarchy" implies a social organization that is imposed from the top. That is not entirely true, however. The lower-ranking individual of a dominant-subordinate pair actually contributes more to the maintenance of a stable social order than the higher ranking individual. About 35 years ago, the animal behaviorist T. E. Rowell correctly stressed that "the subordinate animal ... cautiously observes and maintains a hierarchy, while a dominant one could almost be defined as one which does not 'think before it acts' in social situations."[16] Why should he? A dominant horse doesn't have to worry about a subordinate. On the other hand, a subordinate doesn't want to offend a higher-ranking horse and risk retaliation. Theoretically, that means that once you solidify dominance over a horse, your job essentially is done. The horse will naturally continue to adhere to his role as your subordinate. Nevertheless, in practice, there are certain things that you should do to make sure that your status doesn't decay.

For one, it is important that you always behave like a dominant individual and not like a subordinate when interacting with the horse. If you can convince a horse that you outrank him by acting as if you do, it shouldn't be surprising that you also can convince him that you are his subordinate by acting like one. Most importantly, keep in mind that it is the lower ranking horse that withdraws from the higher-ranking individual and not the reverse. It is a principle that is easy to overlook during routine interactions with a horse.

I can give you an example that I personally encounter frequently. After riding, I often stand with my horse while he grazes. Sometimes, as he nibbles the grass, he moves a little closer to me than I prefer. My natural inclination is to move back a step or two to give him some room. After all, this is meant to be a period of relaxation and reward before he goes back to his paddock. But, contrary to my inclination, I do not give way to him. If I did, for all practical purposes, I would be withdrawing to give him unimpeded access to a resource, the grass—I would be acting like a subordinate. Consequently, rather than stepping back, I gently ask him to withdraw a step or so. It isn't a big thing;

I just give a subtle signal, he moves away and then we both go back to what we were doing.

There are many similar situations that occur routinely while handling horses. For example, I often see people move or even get bumped out of the way when a horse that is tied swings his hindquarters around toward them. Maybe the horse just wanted to look in a different direction. But, remember it is the dominant individual who stands where he wants to stand; space is an important resource to horses. Rowell described a dominant animal "as one which does not 'think before it acts' in social situations."[17] When a horse swings his hindquarters into you, he certainly has not given proper consideration to your higher rank and you have every right to be offended. Obviously, you can't just stand there and get stepped on or bumped; sometimes it's prudent to get out of a horse's way. However, as soon as you can do it safely, remind the horse of your higher rank by telling him to move his hindquarters away from you—pronto. A higher-ranking individual has proprietary rights to all resources, including space. That means you should be able to stand where you want to stand and walk where you want to walk. Don't jeopardize your status by relinquishing those rights by allowing the horse to crowd you or bump into you *under any circumstances*. If he does, don't punish him or treat him harshly, just remind him of your higher rank by asking him to withdraw expeditiously. If you deal with such situations properly, each one quietly helps to keep the horse respectful and cooperative. If you deal with them inappropriately or overlook them entirely, each incident ever so slightly erodes your status and increases the likelihood that the horse will treat you disrespectfully.

I also do not allow my horses to walk away from me at will. I consider it disrespectful. If you saw the movie *Gladiator* you surely remember the scene where The Spaniard intentionally turned his back on the Emperor to express his contempt. I don't feel nearly that strongly about it. It isn't a blatant insult. Even so, it is a sign that the horse thinks there is something more important than me to attend to. It's a mild act of disregard. So when it happens I call him back to me using the attention cue. But I don't expect horses to pay attention to me all of the time. When appropriate, I walk away from them or I tell them to move away from me with a specific cue. In either case, I do it casually; horses readily learn to discriminate when it's OK to go about their business and when it's not.

On Aggression

It seems like there is always one exception to every rule. There is even an old saying, "The exception proves the rule"—whatever that means. When it comes to treating horses with tact and gentleness, the standing exception for many people is when horses bite or kick or try to do so. Then, it seems OK to be harsh with the horse. Some trainers even advocate losing your temper and attacking the horse for a brief period of time. I adamantly disagree with that advice. I devoted quite a bit of the foregoing chapter to convincing you that punishment is not an effective method for eradicating undesirable behavior. That principle holds true whether you are trying to suppress a spontaneous change of gaits under saddle or aggression directed toward you when you are handling horses from the ground. Punishment, at best, only suppresses undesirable behavior temporarily, and it can produce severe negative side effects as well.

The key to dealing with aggression tactfully lies not in counterattacking, but in recognizing it as an extreme example of incivility. Then, the solution becomes apparent: Like other types of incivilities, kicking and biting can be suppressed efficiently, permanently and tactfully by teaching the horse that you are his social superior. Moreover, the higher your rank is perceived to be by the horse, the less likely he is to aggress against you. That means, as you progress through the training described in the preceding sections from establishing your dominance to becoming the horse's leader, you are likewise eradicating any tendency the horse might have to be aggressive toward you.

Rebellion Under Saddle

I would not say in all cases, but many times the horses that behave the most obstinately disobedient or violently rebellious under saddle are those that do not recognize any other individual, whether it be human or horse, as their social superior. Thus they are accustomed to doing what they want to do and going where they want to go. Consequently, they are inclined to rebel, sometimes audaciously, when asked to do something that is disagreeable to them under saddle. They aren't defiant all of the time, but such horses erupt frequently enough to make riders apprehensive about getting on their back.

This is another instance where a marked, often amazing, improvement in behavior accompanies the ground training described in the sections above. The tendency to rebel under saddle diminishes as the horse learns that you are his social superior. I cannot say for certain why the ground work has such a dramatic effect on a horse's behavior under saddle. Maybe they suddenly become aware that they are not always the "king of the mountain" and, therefore, are less inclined to have an emotional eruption when they don't get their way. In any event, the ground work is the safest and most efficient and tactful method that I am aware of for suppressing such behavior.

With such horses, it usually pays to remind them that you are their social superior each time before you mount, at least for a while after the initial training. It doesn't have to be a prolonged lungeing session. I'm not recommending that you wear the horse out before mounting. Just check to make sure he is still respectful of your status by asking him to withdraw a couple of times. If he moves away briskly, don't belabor the issue. If he doesn't, continue the ground work until you get a snappy withdrawal to a subtle cue.

Incivilities That Are Not Sensitive to Social Status

Pestering

Have you ever watched geldings or stallions together in a dry lot? If you have, you probably have seen some of them playing what I call the "mouth game." It's a favorite pastime among geldings that know one another well. Essentially, each horse tries to bite the other horse in the face. They really don't try to bite one another hard; it's just a game, a mock battle of sorts. One feigns an attack while the other tries to evade it and vice versa.

When bored, horses sometimes try to solicit a similar game from handlers by nibbling and nipping at them, mostly with their lips. I see it most often when a handler has been standing for a while holding a horse on a lead rope. I'm not talking about a horse that truly bites or threatens to bite in an aggressive manner. In this case, it just mischievous—annoying and certainly distracting, but not really dangerous. It reminds me of an ill-behaved child who continuously pesters to get his mother's attention when she is trying to talk to someone. The horse is bored and looking for something to do.

Handlers usually respond to such shenanigans by telling the horse to "quit it" or something along those lines. They might also try to give the horse a little swat on the nose at the same time.

Unfortunately, in contrast to what many people assume, horses under these circumstances don't interpret such actions as a reproof. To the contrary, from their point of view, it's a respite from the boredom. Even worse, if the handler tries to swat the horse, then the game is on—they evade the handler's counterattack and then feign another attack of their own. And so the game goes back and forth. It might not be the mouth game exactly, but it's close enough to be entertaining for the horse. Meanwhile, the handler becomes increasingly annoyed.

The fact is, in this case, a handler's reproof not only does not suppress the undesirable behavior, it reinforces and perpetuates it. Essentially, the handler's reaction rewards the horse by giving him exactly what he wants. It is far better to simply ignore the horse under such situations. I'm not saying that you should stand there and let a horse bite you. If he is truly being aggressive, do what you must to curb the attack and then establish your social superiority as described above. But if he is just being a mischievous pest, the practice will not be eradicated through dominance; social status appears to be irrelevant in this case—subordinates solicit games as well as dominant horses. Instead, ignore the horse when he starts to pester. Turn your back on him if necessary. Don't direct any attention toward him whatsoever. In so doing, you put Golden Rule #8 (Undesirable behavior extinguishes if it is not rewarded) into action and erase his motivation for the shenanigans—that is, a relief from his boredom. In time, the horse will stop trying to tease you into the game and will patiently stand by you.

Pawing When Tied

Time and again I hear people yell at horses to stop pawing. Pawing is an uncivil habit, but it is not related to social status. Pawing when tied will not disappear with the training described above. Scolding the horse also won't eradicate it. Oh sure, most horses do stop pawing as soon as they are scolded, but shortly thereafter they start again, and the cycle repeats itself with the person scolding the horse over and over again *ad infinitum*.

Have you ever wondered why horses paw when they are tied? Remember all behavior has a motive. If an undesirable behavior persists or worsens, it is a very good bet that it is being rewarded somehow (Golden Rule #7: Undesirable behavior worsens only if it is rewarded). In this case, horses paw for attention—it's boring for them to stand tied.[18] Then, the handler scolds the horse for pawing and, in so doing, gives him exactly what he wants: a change in the *status quo* and a brief relief from the boredom.

Instead, the next time your horse paws, ignore him. Don't react in any way. Don't yell at him. Don't talk to him. Don't look at him. Don't pet him. Don't do anything at all that is directed toward the horse, and don't let anyone else do anything either. Just ignore him totally. Again, by doing so, you put Golden Rule #8 (Undesirable behavior extinguishes if it is not rewarded) to work. It may take months for the horse to stop pawing entirely, especially if it is a well-ingrained habit. But, in the meantime, all that you have to do is go about your business and ignore him when he paws. What could be easier?

CHAPTER

OVERCOMING FEAR
AND MISTRUST

Have you ever seen a deer in the wild? If you have, I bet you immediately recognized that you had to stay very still and quiet or you would frighten it away. Deer are constantly alert for changes in their surroundings and they react quickly to anything the least bit suspicious. Their survival depends on it.

The same was true for the ancestors of modern horses. Like deer, they were prey animals whose survival depended on a quick reaction to anything out of the ordinary. It was far better to be overly cautious and to flee unnecessarily than to be mistakenly nonchalant about something potentially harmful.

This tendency is still active in modern horses despite thousands of years of domestication and selective breeding.

In the early stages of training, it can be expressed as apprehension about things used to handle, ride or care for the horse or even as a mistrust of the human handlers themselves. But it is a part of the equine nature that must be dealt with to some degree regardless of the horse's level of training and experience. Although some horses are inherently much less reactive than others, they all can be dubious of one thing or another—maybe an object or some type of animal that the horse hasn't seen before or a certain situation. Just as optimizing sensitivity to signals is an ongoing endeavor, so is minimizing sensitivity and reactivity to extraneous stimuli. It is part of the process of taming a horse, of replacing instinctual reactions with responses directed by the handler or rider. Otherwise, there will be recurrent struggles between training and instinct and limitations to what can be done to and with the horse.

It is terribly unjust that we sometimes interpret the finely tuned defense reactions of horses as symptoms of a flawed temperament. Sometimes horses are even punished for this instinctual behavior that has been integral to the survival of their genus for literally millions of years. Punishment and harsh treatment, however, only increase a horse's apprehension. It is unquestionably the wrong thing for a rider or handler to do. Xenophon wrote more than 2,000 years ago "Compulsion and blows inspire only the more fear ...."[19] Instead, the horse must be convinced that his suspicions are unfounded and that the source of concern can be dismissed and ignored in the future. The means for rationally and tactfully accomplishing that goal are implicit to golden rules already discussed in Chapter II for optimizing sensitivity to aids and cues. Optimizing sensitivity to signals and minimizing sensitivity and reactivity to other stimuli are simply two sides of the same coin.

Golden Rules of Desensitization

In past eras, desensitization was often accomplished by a process that has been referred to as "flooding."[20] Even today, some horses are "broke" for riding by this method. Essentially, the horse is forcibly prevented from fleeing while the frightening stimulus is presented full strength. Exposure to the stimulus continues until the horse "gets used to it" or dies from exhaustion or injury. If you have an image of a horse tied up short to a sturdy snubbing post and thrashing about while a weathered cowboy flips a saddle blanket over his back and around his shoulders, you have the right idea. "Sacking out" is one example of desensitization by flooding.

You probably also remember those scenes in old western movies where the crazed horse is held down by a couple of cowhands while a saddle is unceremoniously tossed onto his back. Then, the hero jumps on and rides the bucking horse until he calms down. This is another example of desensitization by flooding, in this case, to the saddle and the rider.

You might also have seen flooding used in a peculiar way with Mustangs. Over the past several years there have been a number of shows on television that featured stories about a "new method" for breaking Mustangs. Essentially, the wild horse was herded into a small chamber where all of the space around and above him was filled with grain. All that remained exposed was the horse's neck and head. Then, while restrained in this manner, the horse was approached, touched, etc. It was presented as a miraculous new solution for getting Mustangs accustomed to the presence of and handling by humans. In fact, it is simply flooding. All that was new is the method of restraint.

In any event, flooding continues to be used and reappears in new forms because it works. Why? The answer is implicit to Golden Rule #2 which says, "A signal should stop as soon as a horse begins to make an acceptable response." If it does not, the horse will become less sensitive to the signal. Golden Rule #9 is merely a generalization of this basic concept:

GOLDEN RULE #9

The Reaction to a Stimulus Will Dwindle if the Stimulus Continues While the Reaction Occurs

In the example of sacking out, thrashing about is the reaction to the saddle blanket, which is the stimulus. Because exposure to the saddle blanket continues despite the horse's reaction to it, the reaction eventually extinguishes. In fact, flooding is a very powerful method of desensitization because the stimulus always continues until the reaction completely stops.

Unfortunately, however, desensitization by flooding is neither gentle nor tactful. Imagine yourself bound to a post while being exposed to and touched by something you truly fear. Whether it's actually harmful or not doesn't really matter. Maybe it's something like a harmless snake or a big, hairy spider, which many people inherently fear. The only thing that is important is that your instincts are screaming for you to run away, but you can't. It is a horrible image, isn't it? It is not surprising that flooding can cause great psychological harm.

Even when things seem to turn out OK, horses that have been treated in this manner often lack affect and perform in a mechanical sort of way without enthusiasm.[21] Of course, there is also an obvious potential for the horse or the handler to get hurt during flooding. It is a primitive and brutal method. Even though it adheres to a golden rule of training, there is no justification for using it.

This, however, should not be interpreted as a condemnation of Golden Rule #9 itself. Do not confuse a golden rule with a method that utilizes it. As you will see below, there are times and situations where Golden Rule #9 can be useful when applied more gently and tactfully than during flooding. However, Golden Rule #3 (Signals should never be ignored) holds the key to a much more broadly applicable fundamental of desensitization.

In the discussion of how to implement Golden Rule #3, I said, "When a signal terminates before a horse responds, it tends to make him less sensitive to the signal." Once again, this adjunct of a rule for optimizing sensitivity to signals can easily be reformulated as a rule for desensitization:

G O L D E N   R U L E   # 1 0

The Reaction to a Stimulus Will Dwindle if the Stimulus Terminates Without the Reaction Occurring

The trick to implementing this golden rule is to find a way to expose the horse to the frightening stimulus without the unwanted reaction occurring.[22] Actually, there are two different ways to accomplish this goal. Each method is more appropriate for certain types of situations than for others. The crucial factor is whether or not the potency of the stimulus can easily be manipulated, that is, increased and decreased.

Manipulating Stimulus Potency

Kell B. Jeffery was a legendary horse trainer from Australia. The story of how Mr. Jeffery became involved with horses and the method he discovered for training them is both fascinating and instructive. Here is a brief overview as told by one of his disciples, Maurice Wright.

> On the occasion of his visit to Guyra in 1953, Mr. Jeffery told us that it was at a place not far east of that township near Chandler's Peak, that he first conceived the idea of a humane approach to animals, and where he first made close contact with horses. He told us that he had been studying law at the Melbourne University

when he suffered a collapse, and his doctors had ordered him into the country, so he came to Guyra to recuperate. He could not ride and had no previous experience with horses. As he recovered his strength he became bored with his surroundings and began to look for some way to occupy his time. The property was a big cattle run, and the men spent most of their time on horseback, and were away from the station for days on end.

There were a lot of horses on the property and they soon became a source of interest to this bored young man .... There was one mare in particular that was especially attractive to him and he noticed that she was not being worked with the others. To satisfy his curiosity he asked the boss why this was so, and he was told that she was unbroken. Apparently somebody had tried to break her and she had proved too difficult for him. She was a beautiful mare and he fell in love with her.

One day when the men had saddled their horses at dawn and as usual he had watched them ride away, he noticed the mare feeding near the yard. He crept round behind her and managed to drive her through the big gate .... He told us that at this stage he had no idea what he was going to do, but he thought that if he could only gain her confidence she would let him handle her .... At the end of the day when the men returned home they were amazed to see this wild mare being ridden around the big yard by the delicate lad with only a rope around her neck. Mr. Jeffery said himself that he could remember being astonished at how quickly she responded, and how she had accepted him. Once she had gained

confidence with him she allowed him to do almost anything that he wished with her, as though she wanted to
do the right thing for him. He told us that she became
very quiet with him and that he learned to ride on her ....
The old man told us that he did not at the time realize
what he had done, because as he had never previously
seen a horse being broken, he had not been indoctrinat-
ed with the traditional rough breaking techniques, so he
thought that he was using the usual approach." [23]

Mr. Jeffery began public demonstrations of his method for
training horses sometime around 1914. For the next 35–40
years, he continued to give demonstrations throughout the
eastern states of Australia. He "always insisted that he would
not make a horse submit to him. He always said the horse
must be persuaded in these matters and never forced."[24]
Here is a description of a demonstration given by Mr. Jeffery
in Guyra in 1953:

Here, before a large and skeptical crowd, he demon-
strated his method by handling and quietening a ten-
year-old gelding which had been given up by previous
horse-breakers. This horse was a confirmed kicker, and
when yarded before he was caught he seemed to be
occupying his time by kicking at the rails and anyone
who ventured too close. It seemed a highly dangerous or
even impossible task for anybody to catch and handle
this horse without putting him in a crush. At this time
Mr. Jeffery was said to be 75 years old and suffering from
a weak heart. He seemed too frail and old to tackle any
unbroken horse, let alone this old outlaw.

He had the horse roped by one of the stockmen who

rode in on a quiet horse and passed the rope around the horse's neck. The old man immediately took the rope and ordered his offsider out of the yard .... in no time he seemed to have the horse mesmerized to the stage where he could handle most of his body and legs without any sign of resistance or fright on the horse's part.

He then called for a four gallon oil drum which he placed beside the horse. Having handled the horse's back he then proceeded to climb on the drum, which capsized, throwing the old man at the horse's heels. To every-body's amazement the horse hardly turned a hair. From then on he proceeded with his handling and mounting technique before an incredulous crowd. Nobody, includ-ing myself, could see how all this could be achieved without some kind of tranquilizing or hypnotism.[25]

What Mr. Jeffery had discovered was neither a magical elixir nor animal hypnosis. It was a method for desensitizing hors-es that takes advantage of Golden Rule #10 (The reaction to a stimulus will dwindle if the stimulus terminates without the reaction occurring). He had inadvertently found a way to expose the horse to what was perceived to be a threatening stimulus, in this case it was Mr. Jeffery himself, without a fear reaction occurring. By doing so, the horse's sensitivity and reactivity to Mr. Jeffery's presence and handling dwin-dled and his confidence that Mr. Jeffery would do nothing to harm him grew.

Approach and Retreat

At the heart of Mr. Jeffery's method of breaking horses was a procedure that came to be known as "advance and retreat."

Basically, Mr. Jeffery desensitized horses to his presence and handling by repeatedly advancing toward the horse and then retreating just before the horse reacted. An analogy might help to explain why this leads to desensitization:

Have you ever been driving on a two-lane road with a car in the distance coming toward you in your lane as it passes another car? What went through your mind? When it happens to me, I wonder whether the car will get back into its own lane before it reaches me or whether I will have to take some evasive maneuver. I recognize that the car is potentially dangerous to me, but I don't take any action immediately. Instead, I simply continue to assess the situation. I make a decision to wait and see what happens. Eventually, the car either will get back into its own lane or, at some point as it grows closer, I will take evasive action.

A horse is presented with a similar situation when he is exposed to what he perceives to be a threatening stimulus at a distance. The horse recognizes the potential danger but he also recognizes that, as yet, there is no need to take action. He stands his ground and assesses the situation, waiting to see what happens. If the stimulus continues to approach, at some point the horse will react to it. If the stimulus goes away, retreats in Mr. Jeffery's case, before it reaches that reaction point, it confirms to the horse that his decision to wait and see what happens was correct. It reinforces, that is, strengthens, his conviction that it is unnecessary to react to the stimulus. With each successive exposure, that conviction becomes stronger. As a result, Mr. Jeffery was able to get a little closer to the horse each time he advanced. Eventually, Mr. Jeffery could touch the horse before retreating. Then he could touch the horse for progressively longer periods of time and over a greater extent of the horse's body. And so the progression continued until Mr. Jeffery could touch any area on the horse and sit on his back without alarming him. It's a marvelously gentle and tactful alternative to desensitization by flooding.

Furthermore, the method of "advance and retreat" is adaptable to a variety of situations. As a general rule, it can be used to desensitize horses to anything that can easily be moved toward and away from them, like the handler himself or objects including any type of tack, winter blankets, electric hair clippers, ropes, grooming vacuums, rain gear, plastic bags, etc. It can also be used to desensitize areas on the horse's body that are particularly sensitive to touch, perhaps the head, legs, belly, udder, sheath, etc. In such cases, the "advance" is from an insensitive area of the body toward the sensitive area. For a head-shy horse, for example, one could run a hand, let's say, from the base of the neck toward the head, progressing a little farther each time before withdrawing. It is a versatile method that pays great dividends in the long run. Not only will the horse learn to ignore the stimulus, but also, with each new fear that you help the horse to conquer, his trust in you will grow. In time, he will accept new things casually, confident that you will not do anything to harm him.

When applying the advance-and-retreat method, it is important to advance each time to a point just below the horse's threshold for reacting. The reaction you will be trying to extinguish will be one of evasion. Be alert for any sign that the horse is about to move away from the stimulus.

Usually, he will begin to glance away from the stimulus, tense his muscles, maybe raise his head, and certainly he will begin to lean away from the stimulus just before he has made the final decision to move away. As soon as you see such signs, immediately withdraw the stimulus. *Just as the release of an aid is rewarding when riding, so is the withdrawal of a stimulus that arouses even slight apprehension.* In this case, the reward strengthens the horse's conviction that it is unnecessary to react to the stimulus.

The sign of an effective "retreat" is relaxation. Do not begin another advance if the horse is not completely calm and relaxed. It helps if you literally turn your back on the horse when you retreat, but it isn't always necessary. You might even want to walk the horse for a brief period. Be casual. Divert your attention from the horse. If there is another person in the vicinity, chat with him or her for a moment or so if appropriate. Or briefly watch someone else handle or ride his or her horse. The retreat is more than the simple withdrawal of the stimulus. It should be a psychological break in the action, a period when the horse can take a deep breath and regain his composure.

As a general rule, the greater the horse's initial anxiety, the longer desensitization takes. You cannot rush the process. The horse sets the pace. Each time you advance you must withdraw before the horse begins to move away from the stimulus. Try very hard not to exceed that threshold. The horse will tell you his limitation by showing signs that he is thinking about moving away. Remember, to comply with Golden Rule #10, the horse must be exposed to the stimulus without the reaction occurring.

If you unintentionally advance too far or too quickly before retreating and the horse moves away, desensitization will be delayed—it's a breach of Golden Rule #10 (The reaction to a stimulus will dwindle if the stimulus terminates without the reaction occurring). However, should this occur—and it is likely to occasionally—all is not lost. There are a couple of things that can be done to minimize the damage. First and foremost, make sure you do not become frustrated with the horse. The mistake was yours; do not punish the horse and add to his apprehension. Remember, he is simply following ancient instincts.

Second, this is a time when Golden Rule #9 (The reaction to a stimulus will dwindle if the stimulus continues while the reaction occurs) can be used effectively. Instantly, switch temporarily from a mental mode that is focused on Rule #10 to one that is focused on Golden Rule #9. Remember, according to Golden Rule #9, the "reaction to a stimulus will dwindle if the stimulus continues while the reaction occurs." So, if possible, continue to expose the horse to the stimulus while he is reacting to it. Do the best you can. You might have to use some mild restraint while the reaction is taking place. That's OK as long as it is mild restraint—not so strong that it becomes a struggle between you and the horse or that puts you or the horse in jeopardy of getting injured. Then, when you see some sign that the reaction is stopping, withdraw the stimulus immediately. Be generous in your interpretation. Accept the slightest indication that could be interpreted as the waning of the reaction. If, on the other hand, more than mild restraint is required to continue exposure, withdraw the frightening stimulus, give the horse some time to calm down and relax, and then present it again, advancing a little more carefully this time. Make sure you do not pass the horse's reaction point.

Length of Exposure

Actually, the name "advance and retreat" is a little misleading. There is more to it than simply changing proximity to the horse. More importantly, advancing toward a horse and retreating from him is a way to change the potency of a frightening stimulus. The more potent a stimulus is, the more likely it is to elicit a response. Advancing a frightening stimulus toward a horse increases potency, and retreating decreases potency.

Another factor that can affect the potency of a frightening stimulus is length of exposure. The longer a frightening stimulus is present, the more likely it is to elicit a reaction from a horse. This principal is as important to understand as "advance and retreat" itself. In fact, it was a key element in Kell Jeffery's method of breaking horses. Remember that "eventually, Mr. Jeffery could touch the horse before retreating. Then, he could touch the horse for progressively longer periods of time ...." Clearly, Mr. Jeffery intuitively appreciated that the amount of time that he touched the horse was no different, in principal, than physically advancing toward the horse. In both cases, there is a threshold of tolerance—a point at which the horse will react to the stimulus. To comply with Golden Rule #10 (The reaction to a stimulus will dwindle if the stimulus terminates without the reaction occurring), the horse's exposure to the stimulus must stop before reaching that point.

The length of exposure is important for other types of frightening stimuli as well. For example, before desensitization, a saddle pad, winter blanket, plastic bag, etc., that touches the horse for a split second is less likely to elicit an evasive reaction than one that touches him for a longer period of time. But, the principal is not limited just to touch. It applies to all other types of frightening stimuli as well. In addition, although length of exposure often can be used in conjunction with approach and retreat, it also can be useful in its own right. For example, initially some horses worry about being sprayed with such things as fly spray or coat conditioners. In such cases, it makes no sense to advance and retreat, but you can vary the length of exposure. Start with a single, brief squirt and work toward more prolonged, repeated sprays. Between squirts, allow the horse to relax. Don't keep pointing the spray bottle at the horse; drop it to your side. Give him a clear period of relief from the frightening stimulus.

I recently used length of exposure to desensitize a horse to a sound. As I was riding, I stopped and gave the horse an opportunity to graze along a fence line. All was well until the horse moved a little to reach a nearby morsel of grass. When he did, the whip that I was carrying dragged along the fence and the sound that it made spooked him; he didn't go far, just a few steps. As soon as he calmed down, I rode him back to the fence line and allowed him to graze. When he was calmly grazing, I intentionally rubbed the whip along the fence; he spooked again. I rode him back to the fence. This time, I tried to make the rub a little shorter. It wasn't short enough; he spooked again. I repeated the sequence. This time, I only tapped lightly on the fence. The tap got his attention but he didn't spook; the length of exposure to the frightening stimulus—the sound made by the whip on the fence—was below the horse's threshold for reacting. After a moment, I tapped again and so on, each time making sure that the horse was calm before I tapped. After a while, I found that I could tap a number of times in a row without causing a reaction. Eventually, I was able to drag the whip very briefly along the fence without eliciting a response. Then, I could drag it for a little longer. Eventually, the horse became totally desensitized to the sound of the whip dragging on the fence.

After the initial trial and error to find a sound that was below the horse's threshold for reacting, anyone watching while I desensitized the horse would probably have concluded that I was merely playing absent mindedly with my whip while the horse calmly grazed. Remember Maurice Wright's statement about Mr. Jeffery's demonstration: "Nobody, including myself, could see how all this could be achieved without some kind of tranquilizing or hypnotism."[26] It is an exquisitely subtle technique that is easy to apply and not taxing to either the horse or the handler. The trainer should be casual and nonchalant, and the horse should remain calm and relaxed during the entire process.

Changing Physical Attributes

The potency of a frightening stimulus also can be manipulated by changing its physical attributes. Here are some rules of thumb:

> *SIZE*: Potency usually decreases as the size of a frightening stimulus is reduced. For example:

- A saddle pad, winter blanket, tarpaulin, plastic bag or the like that is made smaller by being folded is less likely to be frightening than an unfolded one.

SOUND: Generally speaking, the more sound that a frightening stimulus makes, the more likely it is to frighten the horse. For example:

- Hair clippers are more likely to elicit a reaction when they are turned on than when they are turned off.

- The louder a piece of plastic is crinkled, the more likely it is to elicit a reaction from a horse.

- A firearm that is fired is obviously more likely to elicit a reaction than one that is silent. Of course, the louder the sound of the shot, the more likely it will cause a reaction.

MOVEMENT: Typically, the more a stimulus moves and the faster it moves, the more likely it is to cause a reaction. In addition, the more irregular the movement, the more likely it is to frighten a horse. In fact, rhythmic movement tends to calm horses, whereas arrhythmic movement tends to excite them. For instance:

- A saddle pad, winter blanket, plastic bag, etc., that is held still is less likely to cause a reaction than one that is shaken about. One that is moved rhythmically is less likely to cause a reaction than one that is moved in an irregular manner.

- A rope that is twirled is more likely to elicit a reaction than one that is not.

- A lead rope that is repeatedly tossed across a horse's back in rhythm is less likely to cause a reaction than one that is tossed at irregular intervals.

STRUCTURAL COMPLEXITY: In general, the more structurally complex the frightening stimulus is, the more likely it is to cause a reaction. For example:

- A hair clipper with an electrical cord attached is more likely to elicit a reaction than a battery-operated, cordless clipper.

- A Western saddle with all of its rigging is more likely to cause a reaction than an English saddle.

Often it is advantageous to modify the physical attributes of the stimulus in combination with the advance-and-retreat method and/or when desensitizing a horse by manipulating the length of exposure. In the initial stages of desensitization, make the stimulus as physically innocuous as possible: fold it up, make it structurally simple, keep it quiet or use some other means to reduce the potency of the frightening stimulus. Then, desensitize the horse to it by advancing and retreating and/or by manipulating length of exposure. When the horse is desensitized to the weak stimulus, increase its potency in small steps by modifying its physical attributes—the smaller the steps the better.

Try to control the potency of the frightening stimulus by all of the means possible. In the example given above where the horse was desensitized to the sound of the whip on the fence by manipulating time of exposure, I initially tapped very lightly on the fence with the whip and kept the movement of the whip to a minimum. Then as the horse became desensitized, I gradually increased the level of sound and the amount of movement made by the whip. Only when the horse was insensitive to taps that were made with a moderate level of sound and fairly normal whip movement did I begin to try making multiple taps. When I did, I again progressed from light taps to stronger taps. In addition, I tapped rhythmically rather than arrhythmically.

There are multiple dimensions by which stimulus potency can be controlled. The more ways you utilize, the better. It allows you to increase the potency of the stimulus in small steps while always staying below the horse's threshold for reacting to it. *Desensitization is a process that goes more quickly when you proceed slowly.* Eventually, the horse will be calm and relaxed in the presence of the stimulus, even when it is presented at full strength.

But don't stop there. Solidify the training even further by continuing the process of desensitization. If you want a horse to be completely calm and relaxed in the presence of what once was a suspicious or frightening stimulus, don't stop training when you reach the initial goal. Make the training dead solid. Make sure the horse will not react to the stimulus no matter what happens. Take a winter blanket, for example. Your goal probably would be to have the horse remain calm while you put it on and take it off him. However, if you stop training at that point, you might be unpleasantly surprised at the horse's reaction sometime later when you inadvertently drop the blanket or nonchalantly shake it to remove debris. *Train for exceptional circumstances.* Desensitize the horse as thoroughly as possible. You should be able to shake the blanket vigorously while standing beside the horse, toss it onto his back, slip it over his head, drop it beside him, etc. Ultimately, you should be able to do anything with the blanket without the horse reacting.

CHAPTER

VI

DISPELLING FEAR, ANXIETY AND TENSION UNDER SADDLE

I will tell you at the outset that it is not easy to desensitize a horse to frightening stimuli while riding, and the more reactive the horse is to his surroundings, the more difficult the task. Often, even experienced riders try to curb spooking and shying by restricting the amount or nutritional quality of the horse's feed or by giving concoctions that purportedly calm horses. Others lunge their horses to tire them out before mounting. There are even individuals who lightly tranquilize their horses before riding. Sometimes these approaches do make horses less reactive to their surroundings, but, often, they are detrimental to the horse's physical and mental well being over the long run. They can also diminish endurance, interfere with training and even make the horse unsafe to ride.

Usually it is not possible to control the potency of a frightening stimulus when you are mounted. Unless you have an assistant on the ground, you are not likely to have any control whatsoever over its physical attributes. You also cannot modify the potency of the stimulus by moving it toward and away from the horse. You could take the horse closer to the frightening stimulus and then turn him around and ride away, but that is not the same. At first blush, it might seem like an inconsequential difference, but riding a horse toward and away from a frightening stimulus is, in fact, entirely different than moving a stimulus toward and away from the horse, as per the approach and retreat method described in Chapter V. Horses normally react to a frightening stimulus by moving away from it. Therefore, if you ride a horse away from the stimulus, you are merely accommodating and reinforcing his inclination to avoid it.

If you cannot manipulate the potency of the frightening stimulus, then the only other option is to deal with the horse's reaction itself. To comply with Golden Rule #10 (The reaction to a stimulus will dwindle if the stimulus terminates without the reaction occurring), the reaction to the stimulus must be prevented or at least moderated in order to desensitize a horse. However, the method by which this is accomplished is of paramount importance. It is not simply a matter of forcibly restraining the horse from fleeing; that would be desensitization by flooding as discussed earlier. Instead, the primary goal should be to moderate the intensity of the reaction to the suspicious or frightening stimulus. The best way to do that is by averting muscular tension within the horse. That is not to say that you should allow the horse to flee. But your first thought, if not reaction, should be to neutralize all muscular tension.

Muscular Tension

Frightening stimuli trigger both mental and physical changes. Muscular tension is part of the physical response: it prepares the horse for explosive actions, thereby heightening his ability to react quickly to the frightening stimulus and to adjust rapidly to changes in the situation.

I'm sure that you have experienced the muscular tension that accompanies apprehension or fear. If you are like me, you sit tensely in the dentist chair in preparation for that sharp pain that might come at any moment. Maybe you are afraid of heights or enclosed spaces. If so, you certainly can recall the tenseness you have felt when you were unavoidably subjected to such situations. You might also have experienced it late at night when you were sitting alone in a quiet house and there was an unexpected noise from an unknown source. Or maybe you can recollect that feeling of muscular tension that occurred when you nearly had a car accident. In the extreme, the tension can leave you frozen with fear. Nevertheless, it is an integral part of the fight-or-flight reaction, and it occurs automatically without conscious thought.

Muscular tension normally results from opposing muscles working against one another. For example, you can tense your arm by simultaneously activating both the triceps and the biceps of the upper arm. Horses likewise have opposing pairs of muscles. In fact, most skeletal muscles are organized in opposing pairs. When a muscle bends a joint, there must be an opposing muscle to unbend it. However, horse and rider represent a unique state of affairs. The muscles of the horse and those of the rider can also work against one another. The horse tries to evade the frightening stimulus and, in an attempt to prevent it, the rider braces against him, producing tension and stiffness in both horse and rider. Muscular tension, therefore, can be caused by the natural activation of opposing muscles within the horse or by the muscles of the rider bracing against those of the horse.

Regardless of the source, tension is a major component of the fear reaction. In addition, it precipitates other physical changes that we associate with fear. Tight, activated muscles require more oxygen than relaxed muscles. As a result, a number of physiological changes take place to fulfill the heightened need for oxygen. Initially, there is a sharp intake of breath, and blood pressure and blood flow to the muscles increase. Then, the horse begins to breathe more rapidly to get more oxygen into the blood, and his heart rate accelerates in order to deliver oxygen to the muscles faster. When muscular tension is lessened, the heightened requirement for oxygen is curbed and the need for rapid breathing and a pounding heart is eased. In essence, several major physical reactions to the frightening stimulus are reduced. This, in turn, dampens the emotional response to the frightening stimulus.

If you took introductory psychology in high school or college, you might remember something called The *James-Lange Theory of Emotion*. Formulated by William James and Carl Lange in the late 19th century, the theory asserts that feelings of emotion, such as fear, are caused by feedback from changes in skeletal muscle tone and peripheral physiology. Accordingly, a frightening stimulus causes certain bodily changes—skeletal muscles tense, heart rate increases, breathing accelerates, etc. It is the perception of those changes that is the emotion or, in other words, the fear. Averting the muscular reaction to a frightening stimulus then not only dampens the physical responses, but in so doing, the emotional response to the stimulus as well. Although The *James-Lange Theory of Emotion* has never actually been proven or refuted, there is little doubt that releasing muscular tension leads to desensitization. It, at least partially, adheres to Golden Rule #10, which states that the reaction to a stimulus will dwindle if the stimulus terminates without the reaction occurring. In this case, it might not totally prevent the fear reaction, but alleviating muscular tension certainly reduces its intensity.

Four Ways to Reduce Muscular Tension

Relieving Muscular Tension by Riding "On the Bit"

The most sophisticated and by far the most effective way to minimize muscular tension is to ride the horse "on the bit." Unfortunately, the phrase "on the bit" is rather vague and often interpreted differently depending on style of riding and level of expertise of the rider. In this case, however, I am referring to a very specific condition: a horse that is "on the bit" is a horse that is longitudinally stretched. This occurs only when the dorsal ligamental system that runs along the horse's topline from the poll to the dock of the tail is fully extended.[27]

A longitudinally stretched horse has an arched neck and a flexed poll as a result of the "neck-telescoping gesture" that has been eloquently described by Dr. Deb Bennett.[28] The neck is supple and ideally should feel as if it is hanging from a cable that is anchored to the rider's seat. The haunches are tucked under and the back is elevated and rounded, allowing it to swing freely from side to side in harmony with the gait. Furthermore, the muscles of the forelegs and hindquarters are toned but relaxed, making the joints of the limbs elastic.

In many respects, a frightened horse is the polar opposite of a horse that is on the bit. Whereas the topline of a horse on the bit is stretched, rounded and supple, that of a frightened horse is contracted, hollow and tense. In addition, the joints of a horse on the bit are elastic and freely moving, while those of a frightened horse are stiff. In fact, the appendicular muscles of a frightened horse sometimes become so tense they visibly quiver. In essence, a horse that is on the bit is the antithesis of a horse that is frightened.

The 19th century British naturalist and evolutionary biologist Charles Darwin recognized the importance of such muscular and postural differences to emotion more than a century ago when he formulated his *Principle of Antithesis*, which asserts that opposite states of mind produce opposite, incompatible postures and movements. For example, think about how different emotions affect our posture and movement. Let's take sad and happy as an example of opposite emotional states. When sad, we slouch and plod along with a frown on our face. But when we're happy we stand erect with a smile on our face and have a bounce to our step. And so it goes, according to Darwin, that opposite emotions pro-

duce opposite postures and movement. Judging by the emotional impact of riding on the bit, the converse also appears
to be valid. That is, producing opposite postures appears to
lead to opposite mental states. Certainly riding on the bit,
when done competently, produces a calm, confident horse.

If you are riding on the bit, a fear reaction such as a
spook, shy, bolt or hesitancy to move forward can be corrected just like any other undesirable behavior. That is, use
the aids to expeditiously return the horse to doing what you
would like him to be doing. Don't dwell on why the horse
reacted; just put him back on the bit and then adjust his gait,
speed and direction as needed.

However, tension often begins to build well before a
horse actually tries to avoid a frightening stimulus. As for
any deviation from the status quo, the earlier you detect and
react to alleviate the tension, the better. Don't wait until the
horse actually makes an evasive maneuver. Your goal should
be to use subtle aids, repeatedly if necessary, to maintain the
horse in a state of physical and mental relaxation. Many
times this can be accomplished simply by regaining the
horse's attention, perhaps with a click of the tongue, a half
halt, a slight vibration of the rein or light taps with the heel
of the foot. Sometimes it helps to bend the horse. A horse
that is bent is less able to brace against the aids than a horse
that is unbent. Some trainers, for example, suggest bending
horses away from frightening stimuli by riding shoulder-in.
It is even more effective if the bend continuously changes.
For example, riding very shallow serpentines can be a very
useful method for warding off muscular tension when riding
on the bit. The serpentines can even be so shallow that they

are imperceptible to onlookers, but make sure that you feel the bend in the horse's body shift from one side to the other as you ride the serpentines; it is during that transition that the horse releases muscular tension. For horses with advanced training, changing the bend back and forth between shoulder-in and haunches-out while keeping the forelegs and hindquarters tracking on the same path can be a very effective way to reduce tension. Use any means you can to thwart the development of muscular tension and prevent the situation from evolving to a point where the horse becomes tense enough to take evasive action.

If, for one reason or another, that is not possible and the horse begins an evasive maneuver, get him back on the bit as quickly as possible. In such situations, it is not necessary to give the horse an opportunity to respond to subtle signals. Just get the job done. A frightened horse will neither eat, drink nor breed. If he won't do things that are basic to his survival and the perpetuation of the species, there is no reason to expect him to obey your subtle signals. On the contrary, it usually requires emphatic aids to elicit a response from a frightened horse. But do not make the situation worse by being harsh. That only exacerbates muscular tension within the horse, thereby increasing rather than decreasing the fear reaction.

If the horse does not respond to your initial signal, try to overcome the resistance as quickly as possible. Do not get stuck bracing against the horse, matching force with equal force; that produces even greater tension within the horse. Also, don't maintain constant leg or rein pressure. Horses quickly become insensitive to signals that don't change. It is much more effective to signal in pulses, with a release of pressure between each pulse. For example, bump with the leg rather than maintaining constant pressure. Rein pressure can be pulsed by squeezing and releasing the fingers; the movement is like that made when squeezing a ball to build up the forearms. Signals that are pulsed are much more conspicuous and less likely to be ignored. Make the release of the aid between pulses definitive; it is often during the release of rein pressure, in particular, that horses relax and go back on the bit. At the same time, don't hesitate to increase the strength of the aid if the horse doesn't respond. Get the horse back on the bit as quickly as you can. Or, if you happen to be riding off of the bit at the moment, maybe you are taking a leisurely trail ride, put him on the bit expeditiously if he shies or spooks at something. Then all of the aids should become silent for a brief moment; harmonize with the horse before adjusting his speed or direction.

It might be helpful to describe certain attributes of a horse that is correctly on the bit and how a fear reaction can affect them:

First, a horse that is correctly on the bit is "straight." The concept of "straight" is easy to grasp once you have experienced it, but it is nevertheless difficult to define. Definitions that describe "straightness" in terms of where the back feet track relative to the front feet or in terms of the curvature of the spine do not take into account all of the circumstances under which a horse can be "straight." A definition that describes straightness in terms of the distribution of the horse's weight might be more comprehensive and consequently more accurate. I suggest that *a horse is straight only when he carries equal weight on his inside and outside legs* (see end note 13). The revered German rider and trainer, Gustav Steinbrecht, hinted at a similar definition in 1884 when he defined "the straight direction in the bend" as "uniform weight on the horse's inside and outside legs."[29] Waldemar Seunig was even more explicit in stating:

> "Even loading on the near and off legs, no matter whether the forehand is more or less stressed than the hindquarters, is the distinguishing feature of correct ... flexion.

> "Any horse that satisfies this condition of even loading on the near and off legs, whether its body is actually a straight line or exhibits a certain flexion of the ribs, is straight."[30]

In any event, the concepts of "straight" and riding "on the bit" certainly go hand in hand. They might even be inseparable. I certainly can conceive of a horse that is "straight" but not longitudinally stretched, but I am not sure that it ever actually occurs for more than a brief moment even in response to a rider's aids. On the other hand, a horse that is longitudinally stretched can easily be straightened. I might even go so far as to say that a fully longitudinally stretched horse *must* be straight. If he is not, then he is contracted on one side or the other and not fully longitudinally stretched.

Second, a horse that is correctly on the bit makes light contact with the bit, and the weight on the two reins is equal. If the contact is not light, the horse is not longitudinally stretched (or the rider has adjusted the reins to an improper length), and the muscles of the horse and those of the rider are working against one another to *produce*, rather than *reduce*, muscular tension. If the weight on the two reins is unequal, the horse is not straight and the muscles of the horse and rider are working antagonistically on the heavier side.

Although it would be impossible to anticipate all of the ways a horse might react to a frightening stimulus, it is safe to say that straightness and light, even contact with the bit are always lost. Typically, a frightened horse comes "above the bit" and becomes hollow on one side (I will refer to this as the inside of the horse), while his center of gravity shifts toward the shoulder on the opposite side (the outside of the horse). Furthermore, he puts excessive weight on the outside rein as he keeps his inside eye on the stimulus. Finally, if the stimulus is behind the horse, he is likely to bolt or at least accelerate. When it is in front of the horse, he is likely to lose impulsion and slow down, perhaps to a halt.

Often the instinctual tendencies of riders under such circumstances are counterproductive. In particular, it is not unusual for riders to be reluctant to use driving aids on a horse that is frightened. It is counterintuitive: It seems illogical to use driving aids when a horse is already bolting or shying, for example. The instinctual reaction is to restrain the horse using the reins. If you have sufficient strength or a big enough curb bit, pulling on the reins might stop a runaway, but it will not put him back on the bit. Often that requires some use of driving aids, which, if the hands do not yield, help to stretch the topline by encouraging the horse to tuck his hindquarters and step farther under his body. This, in turn, also shortens the horse's stride and slows his speed.

It is also common to see riders rely on the inside rein to control horses that are fleeing or shying. It is a natural reaction, for example, to pull on the right rein when a horse flees or shies toward the left. In fact, many riding instructors even advocate circling the horse on the inside rein, making smaller and smaller circles until the horse stops. If your goal is merely to stop a runaway and you are not skilled at putting a horse on the bit, that might be the only thing you can do. However, pulling on the inside rein in this case exacerbates the fear reaction, making the horse even more hollow on the inside and throwing his center of gravity even farther toward the outside shoulder. Consequently, it unbalances the horse and increases the potential for a fall. Finally, some horses are athletic enough to continue to flee even in this awkward position. It is much more effective to put the horse back on the bit, which as discussed below, requires the predominant use of outside rather than inside aids.

There are various methods that can be used to put a frightened horse back on the bit. Some are more appropriate for certain types of horses than for others, and some are more effective under certain circumstances than under others. It would be ludicrous to try to describe all of the potential methods that could be used or the circumstances under which each is most effective. Nevertheless, it seems appropriate to describe two general approaches that are applicable to a variety of situations. In both cases, the primary goal is to straighten the horse. This is usually sufficient in and of itself to put a horse back on the bit. The two methods differ principally in the use of the outside rein.

In the first instance, the outside hand (the hand on the convex side of the horse) is fixed in its normal position. A fixed hand does not pull on the rein but its position does not change due to increased (or decreased) pressure from the horse. It is important that the rider's resistance to increased rein pressure comes from the direction of the rider's outside, not inside, hip. With the hand fixed and the rein properly adjusted in length and stretched, the horse can be straightened most effectively using weight aids—essentially, a lateral wiggle of the rider's hips. The hips are first moved sideways toward the convex side of the horse to bring the rider's center of gravity over the horse's center of gravity. Importantly, the lateral movement of the hips should occur as a result of increased pressure downward onto the inside stirrup; it is as if the hips are pushed over by downward leg pressure. Then the hips are brought back toward the hollow side of the horse with a quick, sharp movement that is sufficiently strong enough to bring the horse's midsection with them. Again, the lateral movement of the hips should be accompanied/generated by downward pressure into the stirrup, the outside stirrup in this case. The pressure into the stirrup should be sufficient to lighten the rider's seat slightly so that the horse's spine can more easily realign. Of course, this must all take place within a split second.

A well-trained horse can be straightened with a lateral weight aid that is so subtle that it is invisible to onlookers. But, in less experienced horses and especially horses that have taken evasive actions, a much more emphatic weight aid is likely to be required. If you are not yet sufficiently skilled to use the weight aid, repeated bumps with the outside calf or heel might also work. This fixed-hand method is generally more applicable when the horse has sufficient or too much forward impulsion, such as when the frightening stimulus is behind or toward the rear of the horse. A fixed hand tends to moderate forward movement as well as helping to put the horse on the bit.

In the second method, the rider's weight (or outside calf or heel) can be used in the same manner as in the first instance, but often it is unnecessary. Usually, the action of the outside rein alone is sufficient to straighten the horse and put him back on the bit if it is raised upward with the rider's elbow fully extended. The rein should be brought straight up, not inward toward the horse's neck. In the extreme, the rider might have to lift the rein nearly to the level of his or her shoulder. At other times, when the reaction of the horse is mild, it might be sufficient to raise the rein by merely rotating the hand so the fingernails are on top. This strategy is most useful when the frightening stimulus is toward the direction of travel and the horse is reluctant to move forward. In contrast to the fixed hand, raising the rein does not block forward movement and even encourages it to a degree.

For both methods, the inside leg is behind the girth to guard against the haunches moving laterally and, if necessary, to help straighten the horse. The inside rein maintains light contact and prevents the neck of the horse from incorrectly bending in response to the outside aids.

Obviously these are reactions that a rider must be able to make instantaneously. Horses can respond to a frightening stimulus in the blink of an eye. It is a time when a rider's reactions should be so thoroughly ingrained from practicing on calm horses that they occur automatically without conscious thought. The longer the rider's response is delayed, the more difficult it is to bring the horse back on the bit.

Relieving Muscular Tension by "Giving to the Bit"

The French trainer François Baucher lived from 1796–1873. He was one of the great, albeit controversial, riding masters of history. Among his contributions, Baucher was the first to recognize that the alleviation of muscular tension in the neck and jaw eased tension throughout a horse's body. Accordingly, he developed an intricate series of rein effects called "flexions" for increasing suppleness.

The Western-style trainer and clinician John Lyons has been the modern day torch bearer for using rein aids to supple and relax horses, and he has written and spoken extensively about what he refers to as "giving to the bit."[31] Giving to the bit is a type of flexion. It is a resistance-free response to a rein cue. For a tense horse to give to the bit, he must release muscular tension in the neck and jaw. Because this, in turn, can relieve muscular tension throughout the horse's body, giving to the bit has the potential to serve as a tool for desensitizing horses to their surroundings.

In contrast to riding on the bit, asking a horse to give to the bit does not require sophisticated riding skills. It is merely a matter of using the reins to signal the horse to change the position of his head and neck or flex at the poll. However, in responding, it is imperative that the horse release all muscular tension in the jaw and neck. The direction and magnitude of the movement is of secondary importance to the release of muscular tension. As a rule of thumb, the most effective way to relieve muscular tension is usually to move the head in a direction opposite to that which the horse moved it. For example, in most cases, horses raise their head when frightened. Therefore, to release muscular tension requires that the head be lowered. On the other hand, if something on the ground causes concern, horses naturally lower their head and stretch their neck toward it. Then the neck must be raised to alleviate muscular tension. If the frightening thing is to the left or right, turning the horse's head and neck in the opposite direction might be the most effective way to relieve tension.

When a horse gives to the bit, weight on the reins essentially should become zero. This requires that the rider's hand does not follow the movement of the jaw and neck when the horse responds to the rein signal. In making the correct response, the horse must be allowed to either escape (earlier in training) or avoid (later in training) rein pressure.[32]

Giving to the bit, as the previous sentence implies, is a learned response. "It takes thousands of repetitions before giving is an automatic response."[33] Even then it is asking a lot to expect a horse that is shying or fleeing to give to the bit. On the other hand, a truly skilled rider can put essentially any horse on the bit under virtually any circumstance. In fact, Baucher's *Effet d'Ensemble*, which entails the horse being longitudinally stretched to the extreme, is even more easily attained in an excited or fleeing horse than in one that is calm and relaxed.[34] That is not to say that giving to the bit is not a useful technique for controlling muscular tension. It simply is of limited use if the situation has developed to a point where the horse begins to make an evasive maneuver.

On the other hand, giving to the bit is highly useful for reducing tension caused by anxiety. Anxiety is similar to fear except it is not relatable to a specific object. It is a vague unpleasant emotional state that stems from feelings of dread, uneasiness, distress, apprehension and the like. Most importantly, anxiety causes muscular tension just like a frightening stimulus. And by doing so, it heightens the propensity of the horse to be reactive to his surroundings. In essence, an anxious horse already is experiencing physiological conditions that are associated with fear. When you are mounted on a horse that is anxious, it can seem as if he is looking for something to be afraid of. Things that normally would be ignored suddenly elicit avoidance reactions.

Have you ever noticed that horses spook and shy more when they are asked to do something that is physically difficult for them or when they are worked hard? It is a common phenomenon that sometimes is taken as evidence that such behaviors are attempts to evade work. This is a misconception. Horses spook and shy more under such circumstances because they are anxious. Likewise, fatigue, illness, injury, separation from the herd or a herd mate, riding alone or under novel circumstances, and insufficient physical or mental exercise can make horses anxious and more prone to spook and shy. These are the times when giving to the bit is most useful. As soon as you feel tension begin to develop, ask the horse to give to the bit. Do it repeatedly if necessary. Once again, treat the muscular tension as any other horse-initiated deviation from what is desirable. Relieve the tension as quickly as possible and as often as necessary to keep the horse calm and muscularly relaxed.

Relieving Muscular Tension Through Leg Yielding

The leg yield is one of the most elementary and versatile lateral movements. It can be used to teach horses to obey sideways driving aids or to teach novice riders how to coordinate aids. For some riding disciplines, the leg yield is merely a stepping stone toward more advanced lateral movements like shoulder-in, haunches-in and half pass. Trail riders use it when opening a gate from the saddle or when trying to avoid banging a knee into a tree that is too close to the path. Leg yielding is not commonly thought of as a means for relaxing horses. However, under certain circumstances it can be used to alleviate muscular tension and, therefore, it carries the potential to desensitize horses to their surroundings.

When a horse leg yields, he moves forward and sideways on two tracks. It can be performed at the walk or trot. A leg yield that is done with the maximal degree of sideways movement is referred to as a side-pass, which can only be performed at the walk. Regardless of the angle of sideways movement or the gait, when leg yielding, the horse's inside legs cross in front of the outside legs, and he is very slightly flexed away from the direction of movement. That is, for a leg yield to the right, the horse's body is slightly curved as if on a very large circle to the left. For a leg yield to the left, the horse is curved as if on a very large circle to the right. It is this slight counter bend that makes leg yielding useful for desensitizing horses.

When horses shy, they bend away from the direction of movement. For example, a horse that shies to the right shifts his center of gravity toward his right shoulder and bends slightly to the left. For a horse that is shying to the

Illustration on facing page: *The leg yield and side pass are lateral movements that can sometimes be used to desensitize horses to their surroundings. In both movements the horse is very slightly bent away from the direction of movement and the inside legs cross in front of the outside legs.*

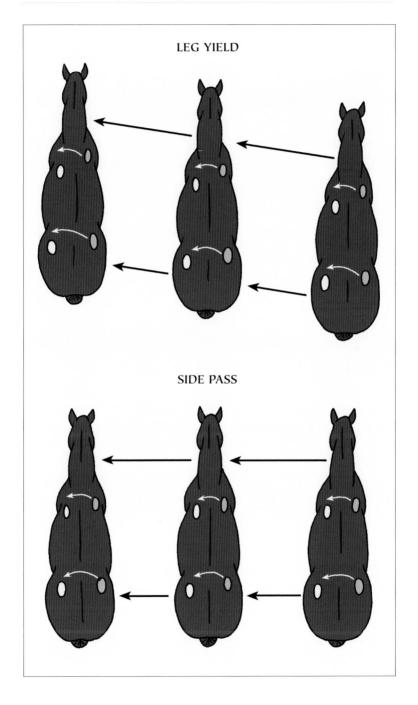

LEG YIELD

SIDE PASS

right to leg yield to the left, that is, back toward whatever it was that caused him to shy, the bend in his body must shift from left to right. For that to happen, muscle tension in the horse's body must release.

Leg yielding is especially useful for desensitizing horses that are ridden in arenas. It is not uncommon, for instance, to see horses shy at doorways and other openings in arena walls. They can also shy when passing viewing areas, mirrors and even mounting blocks. In one local arena, horses often shy away from a corner where jumps are stored. It can be an exasperating problem because it sometimes persists despite the horse's familiarity with the arena and all efforts by the rider to stop it. The leg yield can be a useful method for eradicating shying of this kind.

Here is a general outline of how the leg yield can be used to eliminate shying: As soon as you feel the horse begin to shy, leg yield back to the original path at as steep an angle as possible. The inside leg acting slightly behind the girth should be the predominant aid. The reins should be shifted in unison somewhat toward the direction of movement. The inside rein also can be elevated somewhat to prevent the inside shoulder from escaping. However, the inside hand should not cross over the midline of the horse, and it should not feel as if the horse is being pushed over using the inside rein. Remember, it is a "leg" yield, not a "hand" yield. The

Illustration on facing page: *The figure shows the aids for a leg yield. The aids for a side pass are essentially the same except the rider's weight is shifted more laterally (toward the direction of movement) for a side pass than for a leg yield. Also, if necessary, the hands are more active in restraining forward movement for the side pass.*

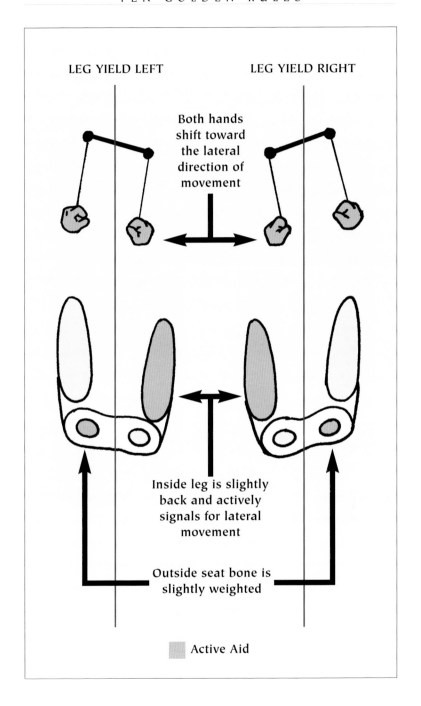

LEG YIELD LEFT LEG YIELD RIGHT

Both hands shift toward the lateral direction of movement

Inside leg is slightly back and actively signals for lateral movement

Outside seat bone is slightly weighted

Active Aid

misuse of the inside rein increases rather than decreases muscular tension by overflexing the neck muscles of the horse. When the horse begins to leg yield, make sure you feel the bend in his body reverse.

At first it is likely that the horse will not respond to the inside leg and will continue to shy away from the stimulus. If that happens, immediately stop the horse. Don't be harsh, but stop him as quickly as possible—before he has passed the stimulus. Then, side-pass back toward the stimulus. When you arrive at the original path, allow the horse some time to stand and relax before proceeding. Do this until the horse obediently leg yields back to the original path without first stopping. With repetition, the horse should become progressively more relaxed and less reactive as he passes the scary place until, eventually, he passes without even taking notice.

Relieving Muscular Tension by Voice and Petting

Without a doubt, the most frequently used method for relaxing horses is to reassure them with a soft voice and a gentle stroke with the hand. Unfortunately, it is a very passive approach that affects muscular tension only indirectly, if at all. Consequently, it is a comparatively weak method for reducing muscular tension. Sometimes it helps but, more often than not, it does more to calm the rider than the horse.

I remember a time when I was riding Gabriel across a nearby farm. We were alone, which normally doesn't bother Gabriel in the least. Nevertheless, on this occasion he began to fret. His neck bulled-up and he seemed to grow a foot taller in the front. Then he began to whinny. He called to a farmer a quarter mile away and then to the cows in the next pasture. As we continued along, it didn't seem like he was going to let the issue go, and he continued to whinny to every living thing he spied. I suppose he was asking, "Does anybody out there know me? I'm alone and a little worried." But in all other respects he behaved properly, so I rode on without intervening.

I'm not sure why but I began to wonder about those cowboys of the Old West. Did their horses ever have panic attacks about being alone? Then an image of a cowpoke singing to his horse as he crossed the open prairie came to mind, and I spontaneously began to softly sing one of those old cowboy tunes. To my surprise, Gabriel relaxed immediately; it literally was like magic. I don't know whether my song affected Gabriel directly or whether singing put me more at ease so he could relax. After all, Gabriel is a rather powerful stallion, and the shear magnitude of his whinny can send chills up and down your spine. In either event, there apparently are times when a softly spoke (or sung) word can help to relax a horse.

Nonetheless, a soft voice and a gentle stroke can also be rewarding to horses. As a result, you run the risk of inadvertently reinforcing rather than extinguishing a horse's fear when you speak soothingly or pet him in the presence of a frightening stimulus. Mary Twelveponies goes so far as to say, "Don't ever pet a horse while he is being or acting scared, thinking to calm him down. You are just rewarding him for his fearful actions."[35] In most cases, it is much more effective to control muscle tone directly by using rein, leg and weight aids.

Concluding Remarks

Methods that are used to help horses overcome their fears are often thought of as techniques for relaxing and calming horses. The questions of why and how they work to desensitize horses to their surroundings are usually not addressed, or the reasons given are vague. Be that as it may, if you look closely enough you will see that their common denominator is that they relieve muscular tension. It is the *sine qua non* of all tactful methods for desensitizing horses when the potency of a frightening stimulus cannot be controlled.

When riding, consider muscular tension the enemy. Regardless of its source, work to eradicate it. A horse that is tense is not only more reactive to his surroundings than a relaxed horse, but he is also unbalanced, more difficult to maneuver and his gaits are uncomfortable to ride. In addition, muscular tension puts excessive strain on muscles and joints and makes the horse more prone to injury and arthritis. The elimination of muscular tension should be an ongoing endeavor, a preoccupation—if not an obsession—for a rider. Use any method at your disposal. If you ride on the bit, don't hesitate to ask the horse to give to the bit or to leg yield when appropriate. If one method doesn't seem to be effective, try another.

Unfortunately, many novice riders do not possess the sensitivity to detect muscular tension within a horse or the riding skills to alleviate it. If you are one of those riders, be honest with yourself and chose a horse accordingly. It is quite common to see a poor match between the temperament of the horse and the skill of the rider. Inexperienced riders, in particular, all too often are drawn to hot-blooded horses with tempestuous natures—I call it the "Black Stallion Syndrome." Then they find that controlling the horse is beyond their skill level and they become disillusioned with and even fearful of riding. Instead, find a well-trained, experienced horse to ride, one that is affected little by things that go on around him and that you can ride anywhere and do different things with easily. Muscular tension occurs to some degree in all horses under saddle and, therefore, you will still have ample opportunity for acquiring the sensitivity to detect muscular tension and the skills to relieve it.

CHAPTER

EPILOGUE:
WHEN IT'S FINISHED

It was quite a few years ago, but I still remember a particular incident that happened during my first year of college. I had just finished a game of Ping-Pong when another freshman challenged me to a match. I said, "Sure, let's play." As we were about to begin, he asked me whether I would like to put a wager on the game. I said, "No, not really. Let's just play for fun." But, he wouldn't take "no" for an answer, and I finally agreed to play for some small amount of money—50 cents I believe it was. Then, just before he served the ball he said, "I should warn you that I have read three books on Ping-Pong." "Hmmm," I replied not knowing what else to say. Then, the game was over as quickly as it began; my opponent didn't score a point. Now, you might be thinking that I must have been a pretty good Ping-Pong player, but that wasn't it; I won easily because my well-read opponent had never played the game before—literally. He actually believed that he would play well just because he had read three books on the subject. To his disappointment, he discovered that it isn't that simple. You can't learn to play Ping-Pong just by reading books. It doesn't work that way for riding and handling horses either. Book knowledge is useless without the acquired skill and finesse to put it into action.

With that in mind, I ask you to be patient as you begin to make use of the 10 golden rules and methods described in this book. Too frequently, people form unrealistic preconceptions about the amount of time it should take to become proficient with new skills. Then they become frustrated when things don't go as smoothly or as rapidly as they expected. Just keep working at it and let the journey take as long as it takes.

Along the way, expect some twists and turns in the road. Often, the first attempts at implementing a new method or idea miss the mark. The difference between effective and ineffective training is often no more than a nuance. Don't be disappointed if things don't go exactly as you expect initially. Just analyze your approach and make adjustments if it seems reasonable to do so. "Observe and reflect."[36] Then, experiment. Find out what works and what doesn't work firsthand. It is only through trial and error that you will gain the fine skills needed for efficacious training. And don't be afraid of making mistakes. Even Nuño Oliveira, one of the greatest riders and trainers of all time, candidly admitted to making "countless errors in the training of literally thousands of horses."[37] If you are consistently gentle and tactful, mistakes are always correctable.

I remember a time when I decided, for reasons that are unimportant, to teach Moment to walk forward when I walked forward, stop when I turned to face her and back up when I faced backward and walked toward her haunches. To my chagrin, the next time I tried to mount by turning toward her haunches she backed up. The faster I walked to try to get into mounting position, the faster she went backward. Naturally, there were other riders around that day—these things never happen when you're alone. Those who knew me found the affair highly amusing; those who didn't know me probably thought my horse was poorly trained. In fact, in this case Moment was well trained, but to do the wrong thing.

You might have similar experiences. If you do, don't become impatient or exaggerate their importance; they're just small bumps in the road. Training horses is fraught with surprises, ups and downs, and successes and disappointments. Just keep going; one step, then another. When you run into rough spots, try to figure out where things went awry and lay out a new plan for getting where you want to go. Let the golden rules be your guide. Learn to see how they can be applied to various situations. Can you guess how I solved the problem of Moment backing up when I tried to mount? Approach and retreat (see Chapter V). Moment wasn't backing up because she was fearful, nevertheless, she was reacting to a stimulus that I didn't want her to react to. The cure was to desensitize her to that stimulus using Golden Rule #10 (The reaction to a stimulus will dwindle if the stimulus terminates without the reaction occurring). There is always a rational way to deal with difficulties if you look hard enough to find them while adamantly refusing to be harsh with the horse.

Moreover, keep in mind that horses are not human. I have read and heard people say that horses are not very smart. I don't believe that is so, but this is not the place to argue the issue. Nevertheless, they certainly do not have the learning ability of a human. Think about how long it takes a child to learn the meaning of the spoken and written word. Years until they become competent, right? When you teach a horse to respond in a certain way to a specific signal, he, likewise, is learning a new language. It takes time and often a great many repetitions for a horse to learn to consistently respond to a subtle cue or to stop reacting to something that he inherently fears.

Art and science are often thought of as the opposite ends of some continuum. I don't think that is the case. From personal experience, I know that there is an art to good science. I'm sure that there is also a science to good art. Sculpting the movement and behavior of a horse likewise has elements of both and neither conforms harmoniously to time constraints. Be patient and make the journey fun and stress-free for you and the horse.

Do you remember what Michelangelo said when Pope Julius II asked, "When will you make an end to it?" in reference to the painting of the ceiling of the Sistine Chapel? Refusing to potentially compromise the quality of his efforts by rushing to meet some arbitrary, self-imposed deadline, he simply said, "When it's finished."

GOLDEN RULES OF HORSE TRAINING

1   *Aids and cues are signals for change.*

2   *Signals should stop as soon as the horse begins to make an acceptable response.*

3   *Signals should never be ignored.*

4   *Signals should be distinct.*

5   *A response should be easy for the horse to make.*

6   *Rewards enhance sensitivity to signals only when they immediately follow an acceptable response.*

7   *Undesirable behavior worsens only if it is rewarded.*

8   *Undesirable behavior extinguishes if it is not rewarded.*

9   *The reaction to a stimulus will dwindle if the stimulus continues while the reaction occurs.*

10   *The reaction to a stimulus will dwindle if the stimulus terminates without the reaction occurring.*

END NOTES

[1] *The Art of Horsemanship* by Xenophon, Reprinted in 1993, J. A. Allen & Company.

[2] *ibid.*, p. 55.

[3] *ibid.*, p. 62.

[4] *ibid.*, p. 24.

[5] *Reflection on Equestrian Art* by Nuno Oliveira, pp. 40–41, 1988, J. A. Allen & Company.

[6] *ibid.*, p. 30.

[7] *Principles of Dressage* by Brig. Gen. Kurt Albrecht, p. 21, 1981, as translated by Nicole Bartle, 1993, J. A. Allen & Co. Ltd.

[8] See *François Baucher: The Man and His Method* by Hilda Nelson, 1992, J. A. Allen & Company.

[9] Author's addition.

[10] *Breaking and Riding* by James Fillis, 1902, Reprinted from the original English edition by J. A. Allen & Company in 1986.

[11] *Dressage du Cheval de Selle* by Capt. Marcel Beudant, 1938, as cited in *Reflections on Equestrian Art* by Nuno Oliveira, p. 27, 1988, J. A. Allen & Company.

[12] *There Are No Problem Horses, Only Problem Riders* by Mary Twelveponies, p. xv, 1982, Houghton Mifflin Company.

[13] Horses that are intentionally bent by the rider or handler or that are naturally crooked have a convex side and a concave side. In this book, the convex side is referred to as the "outside" and the concave side is referred to as the "inside" of the horse. The terms "inside" and "outside" do not refer to the position of the horse relative to arena walls or any other feature of the surroundings.

[14] *Oeuvres Complétes*, pp. 8-9, 1854 as translated by Hilda Nelson, In François Baucher: The Man and His Method. p. 65, J.A. Allen, 1992.

[15] I know that it is a little odd to choose mice as an example. I did so because their ritualized, agonistic behavior has been thoroughly studied under strict scientific conditions. Consequently, I'm certain that the posture I describe in the text is one of submission. Also, I spent a great deal of time during the second year of my graduate career watching agonistic encounters between mice and, therefore, it was the first image that came to mind as I was writing. Some of my observations regarding the agonistic behavior of mice are published in the scientific journals *Behavioral Biology* and *Physiology of Behavior*.

[16] Rowell, T. E. Animal Behavior, 1966 (14) 430–443.

[17] *ibid.*

[18] Some horse's chew on hitching posts when tied for the same reason.

[19] *The Art of Horsemanship* by Xenophon, Reprinted in 1993, p. 37, J. A. Allen & Company.

[20] *Influencing Horse Behavior: A Natural Approach to Training*, Dr. Jim MaCall, 1988, p. 53, Alpine Publications.

[21] *ibid.*

[22] By "frightening," I mean any stimulus that disturbs the horse, arouses his suspicions or alarms him. Essentially, it would be any stimulus that has the potential to evoke an evasive response from the horse.

[23] *The Jeffery Method of Horse Handling* by Maurice Wright, pp. 3–4, first published in 1973 by R. M. Williams Pty. Ltd. and reprinted in 1987 by F. Cockington & Co. Pty. Ltd., Port Adelaide, South Australia.

[24] *ibid.*, pp. 7–8.

[25] *ibid.*, p. 27.

[26] *ibid.* p. 8

[27] See *Principles of Conformation Analysis, Volume I,* by Deb Bennett, Ph.D., 1988, Fleet Street Publishing Corporation.

[28] *Principles of Conformation Analysis, Volume II,* by Deb Bennett, Ph.D., 1989, Fleet Street Publishing Corporation.

[29] *The Gymnasium of the Horse* by Gustav Steinbrecht, p. 188, 1884, reprinted by Xenophon Press, 1995.

[30] *Horsemanship* by Waldemar Seunig, p. 119, 1956, Doubleday.

[31] *Perfect Horse*, Volume 2 (6) 3-6, 1997.

[32] See the discussion in Chapter II regarding the significance of always giving a horse an opportunity to respond to subtle signals and the transition in the motivation for responding that occurs as a result.

[33] *Perfect Horseman*, 6 (2) 1997, p. 3.

[34] See *Racinet Explains Baucher* by Jean-Claude Racinet, 1997, Xenophon Press.

[35] *There Are No Problem Horses, Only Problem Riders* by Mary Twelveponies, p. 112, 1982, Houghton Mifflin Company.

[36] Capt. Marcel Beudant, as cited by Nuno Oliveira in *Reflections on Equestrian Art*, p. 30, 1988, J.A. Allen.

[37] *Reflections on Equestrian Art* by Nuno Oliveira, p. 30, 1988, J.A. Allen.